# Uromastyx

*Plus* Other Common Agamids

*By Jerry G. Walls*

lumina
MEDIA

Front and back cover photos by Lindsay Pike.
The additional photographs in this book are by Lindsay Pike, pp. 5, 6, 9–12, 14, 15, 17, 18, 21, 23, 27, 29, 31, 33–40, 44, 46, 48–54; Paul Freed, 30, 56, 57, 59, 61, 66, 68, 70, 72, 76, 78, 80, 82; Zig Leszczynski, 64.

LUMINA MEDIA™
Chairman: David Fry
Chief Executive Officer: Keith Walter
Chief Financial Officer: David Katzoff
Chief Digital Officer: Jennifer Black-Glover
Senior Vice President, Retail: Scott Coffman
Vice President Content: Joyce Bautista-Ferrari
Vice President Marketing & PR: Cameron Triebwasser
Managing Director, Books: Christopher Reggio
Art Director, Books: Mary Ann Kahn
Senior Editor, Books: Amy Deputato
Production Director: Laurie Panaggio
Production Manager: Jessica Jaensch

LCCN: 96-183295
ISBN: 1-882770-87-0

2030 Main Street, Suite 1400
Irvine, CA 92614
www.facebook.com/luminamediabooks
www.luminamedia.com

# CONTENTS

# CHAPTER 1

# UROMASTYX AND THE FAMILY AGAMIDAE

izards long have been popular pets, with many keepers preferring them to snakes and turtles. Some lizards are small, unexciting animals that are easy to keep once you've determined their diet and best habitat; others can be said to be challenging—even *extremely* challenging. Included in this latter group certainly would be the uromastyx (also called spiny-tailed agamids), a group of about fifteen species of dry savanna- and desert-dwelling burrowers found in Africa and western Asia. Uromastyx can be beautiful, gentle pets, but they are notoriously difficult to care for, requiring strict attention to temperature, humidity, and diet. Until recently, they also had the reputation for being virtually impossible to breed.

As a result of dedicated attention from a few keepers in the United States and Europe, uromastyx lizards have reached the mainstream of the hobby. Several species are now easy to find, keep, and breed, and are available as captive-bred specimens. Even beginners can now successfully keep uromastyx, as long as they are able to give their pets sufficient attention.

But uromastyx are just one genus of lizards in a large family—Agamidae—that includes some of the most popular lizards found in pet shops around the world. Though this book is dedicated to uromastyx, we will also take some chapters to explore the other popular agamid lizards. First, though, let's take a few pages to consider just what makes a uromastyx an agamid, and then we'll address what makes them so distinctive in the family Agamidae.

These male Saharan uromastyx—one in orange phase and one in yellow phase—warm their bodies by basking on a rock slab.

## Defining Agamid Lizards

Possibly because the Agamidae is one of the larger families of lizards, with about three hundred fifty species placed in forty-five to fifty genera, it has yet to be studied in detail by modern methods utilizing DNA technologies. Some attention has been given to Agamidae's relationships to the other lizard families, but these findings have been controversial, as we will see.

## General Characteristics of Agamidae

First, just what are agamids? These lizards, along with the chameleons (family Chamaeleonidae), are acrodonts, meaning their teeth are fused onto the crest of their jaws. Pleurodonts, in contrast, have teeth that rest in shallow depressions within grooves along the insides of the jaws. The most familiar pleurodont lizards probably are the anoles and iguanas and their allies (collared lizards, basilisks, curly-tails), which often are considered to be closely related to the agamids. All agamid lizards are indigenous to the Old World—Africa (barely into Europe), Asia, Australia, and New Guinea; most anoles and iguanas are found in the New World—the Americas, including the Galapagos and Caribbean, with a few found on islands near Tonga and Fiji. Curiously, the large island of Madagascar lying east of Africa is home to several iguanid lizards and not the agamids you might expect to have come from neighboring Africa.

Agamids are moderately large lizards with a rather stocky build. On average, individuals are 6 to 12 inches (15 to 30 cm) total length, including the tail, although there are reports of some specimens as small as 3 inches (7.6 cm) long and others as large as 40 inches (a meter) long. The head is large and features large eyes that have well-developed lids and round pupils. The scales generally are fairly large (but sometimes tiny) and often are keeled (feature a raised ridge down the center of each scale) or carry pointed tubercles; commonly, scales of several different sizes (from large to tiny) appear on the back.

The tail usually is long and sturdy, not prehensile; seldom can it regenerate if broken. The limbs are always rather long (though often thin) and carry five digits each with large claws. (Though, rarely, one toe may be smaller or even absent.) Body form varies and may be depressed (flattened from top to bottom) or compressed (flattened from side to side), the differences often being associated with habitat: agamids with depressed-type bodies tend to be terrestrial and often are burrowers, whereas species with compressed-type bodies often are arboreal (living in trees and shrubs).

It's the teeth that make the agamids a family. The teeth are fused onto the tops of the jaws, as mentioned above, and tend to overlap at their bases, forming a continuous sawlike row toward the back of each jaw. These sawlike teeth are extremely efficient for chopping up both animal and vegetable foods. Additionally, many agamids possess specialized teeth in different parts of the jaws (similar to those in mammals) that are lacking in most other lizards. For instance, at the tip of the upper jaw may be a few incisor teeth that can be used for nipping, followed in some cases by a gap and then one or several pointed canine teeth. Behind the canine teeth are elongated, high-crested, molarlike teeth that may have sharp edges; often, these teeth are fused together at their bases, which makes it difficult for a lost or broken tooth to grow back if its neighbor remains intact. Most adult agamids cannot replace teeth that are lost through wear or accident.

In form, the most extreme agamids probably are the gliding lizards of the genus *Draco* and the thorny devil (or moloch) of the genus *Moloch*. Gliding lizards are tree-dwellers (arboreal) and survive on a diet composed almost exclusively of ants and termites, which makes these agamids difficult to keep in the vivarium. These emaciated-looking lizards are instantly recognized by their "wings," which actually are flaps of skin supported by four to seven movable ribs. The wings (technically called the patagia; singular, patagium) can be folded to the sides when the lizard is at rest and then opened to increase the surface area of the lizard as it glides from tree to tree. The Australian thorny devil is a greatly depressed (flattened) desert dweller covered with a multitude of flexible, pointed spines. This lizard's many narrow teeth are set in continuous rows that project horizontally, presumably to help catch large numbers of ants that form this lizard's exclusive diet.

Agamids are found in environments that range from deep deserts to tropical rain forests and in habitats that range from burrows to the tops of tall trees. Many don shades of green or brown with weak (subtle) patterns. Others feature brilliant colors, placing these creatures among the most beautiful of lizards. Agamids have limited abilities to change colors, mostly from darker to lighter shades of the same color—not the rapid, complete changes seen in some chameleons and anoles. Most agamids are microcarnivores (feeding on insects and other small prey) or omnivores (feeding on both animal and plant matter), although many are strictly vegetarian (as are most adult uromastyx). With few exceptions, agamids lay eggs; live birth is uncommon. A few agamids (such as some butterfly lizards of genus *Leiolepis*) are known to reproduce via parthenogenesis, a form of reproduction in which embryos develop without fertilization.

## Relationships

You may have heard it said that if you go back far enough in the fossil record, all animals are first cousins. Indeed, it appears that the ancestors of the agamid lizards gave rise to their chameleon cousins, which are considered to be the agamids' closest living relatives. Compare a typical chameleon from Africa or Madagascar with a specialized agamid such as an anglehead (genus *Gonocephalus*) and the resemblance is easy to see. Both have compressed bodies for life in the trees, crests on the back, and large heads with expressive eyes. Both the chameleon and the agamid can change color to some degree, and the sides of their bodies may be covered with scales of different sizes. All the chameleon species recognized today have several characteristics that easily distinguish them from the agamids. Two characteristics of note concern the toes and eyes. First, all chameleons' toes are fused into groups—each foot has one group of two toes and one group of three toes. Second, all chameleons' eyes are set in conical turrets that can move independently so the lizards can look forward and backward at the same time.

Though these differences seem obvious to us and it seems we'd never really confuse the Agamidae with the Chamaeleonidae, the differences are relatively small specializations that some scientists have considered of little importance in separating the two families. In 1989, two herpetologists (Drs. Darrel Frost and Richard Etheridge) actually combined the agamids and chameleons into a single family, Chamaeleonidae, on the basis that their skeletal features showed that agamids and chameleons are more closely related to each other than either is to the iguanids and their relatives, the family Iguanidae in the broadest

Though not to the same degree as chameleons, uromastyx do change colors. Shown here when warm, this Moroccan (African) uro displays a much brighter pattern than when cool as shown below.

Shown here is the same lizard as above yet in a cool phase.

sense. Fortunately, few herpetologists have accepted this view, and almost all the literature, both technical and hobby related, still considers the agamids as a distinct family based on easily observable characteristics such as the toes and eyes as mentioned above.

## What Makes *Uromastyx* Different?

Once you've seen a uromastyx of any species and age, you are unlikely to ever mistake it for another type of lizard.

### Teeth

Among all the agamids, the species of the genus *Uromastyx* stand out. Most adult uromastyx are vegetarian; internally, they are distinguished by having sacs in the gut that allow them to digest cellulose from plant cells through fermentation, much as a cow digests grass. This dietary requirement for tough plants and seeds is reflected in their teeth, of course. During development, uromastyx embryos have two pairs of incisor teeth at the front of the upper and lower jaws. Soon after hatching, these teeth give way in the upper jaw to a bony downgrowth from the tip of the skull bones (the premaxillae) that develops into a large central cutting tooth. By the time a uromastyx is adult, all traces of the incisor teeth may be gone, with just the visible "beak" of the upper jaw remaining. Behind the beak is a hard, sharp, cutting surface and then a long row of pointed, fused molar teeth with cutting edges. The lower jaw also has strong cutting teeth toward the back. These specialized tooth rows allow a uromastyx to both cut through the toughest plants and crush small seeds, utilizing all the scarce food it finds in its harsh, desertlike, natural habitats.

## Tail and Legs

At first glance, a uromastyx looks a lot like a chuckwalla (genus *Sauromalus*), a familiar large iguanid lizard from the deserts of the United States and Mexico, or even like a spiny-tailed iguana (genus *Ctenosaura*—another group of iguanid lizards from North and Central America). These resemblances are parallelisms, the results of two different types of animals (in families Agamidae and Iguanidae) evolving under the same pressures from their respective environments. Similar to many other large desert lizards, uromastyx have depressed bodies with small heads and have fairly long, thick, and wide tails; their tails are also ringed with enlarged

This ornate uro's bold colors are carried even onto the tail spines.

scales that carry sharp, projecting edges (the spines of the spiny tails). In uromastyx, the spines usually are thickest and longest at the sides of the tail and are absent under the tail; but regardless of details, the tail makes a great club for use against predators. Uromastyx generally have small scales of one size on the back, as well as some enlarged, usually spiny scales on the thighs of the hind legs. These thigh spines can draw blood if you carelessly pick up a uromastyx and get a finger squeezed between a hind leg and the body. All the feet have five digits ending in large claws.

## Head

The tympanum (ear drum) is set deeply into a large ear opening that often has projecting scales at the front edges. The eyes are large, pale to dark brown, expressive, and set between movable lids. The nostrils are circular, usually edged with enlarged scales, and set high on the snout between the eye and tip of the snout. The olfactory sacs inside the snout (which allow the lizard to smell) are large and also are joined by a special gland that removes excess sodium and potassium compounds from the bloodstream. These chemicals are found in foods and are expelled from the nose as white crystals that often form at the edges of the nostrils. If you see such white crystals, don't worry— they are perfectly normal and just a way of removing toxic plant products from the body.

The hollow-looking depression seen on the side of this ornate uro's head is the ear opening.

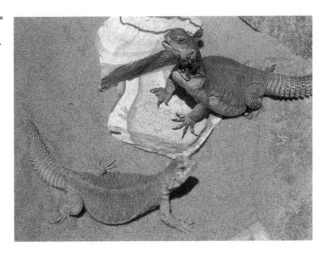

Color tone can vary dramatically depending on subspecies, temperature, mood, and shed cycle. Both of these specimens are Egyptian uros (*U. aegypticus*), yet the one in orange phase stands out dramatically.

## Size and Colors

Uromastyx (which I'll often abbreviate to "uros" in coming pages) are heavy-bodied lizards that range from about 10 inches (25 cm) to at least 30 inches (76 cm) in total length; the tail length usually is half or less of the total length, varying with species. The scales on top of the uro's head are small and seem randomly distributed, seldom forming the complex patterns commonly found in many other lizards. Both males and females have pores on the thighs of the hind legs, though the pores seldom are well-developed except in males of some species. (More about that in chapter 5.) The colors vary greatly, from dull blackish brown without a distinct pattern as seen in the Egyptian uromastyx (*Uromastyx aegypticus*) to bright blue or green with yellow spots (male ornate uros, *U. ornatus*) to bright yellow with contrasting black legs (Mali uros, *U. maliensis*).

# CHAPTER 2

# SELECTION

Uromastyx need lots of room, dry surroundings, and hot temperatures—generally, 120 degrees Fahrenheit (49 degrees Celsius)—to thrive, which means that you must carefully consider whether you can provide any uromastyx with its requirements before you purchase the animal. They are not the easiest lizards to keep; they can be relatively expensive to purchase and to heat, and they are demanding in their needs. However, they also can be among the prettiest large lizards, and they have a distinctive "teddy bear" type of personality that people find appealing.

## Captive-Bred Versus Wild-Caught
For the reasons explained below, you should buy a captive-bred uro if possible. Captive-breds may be available from your pet shop, a herpetological exposition, or a breeder (through advertisements in magazines or on the Internet). However, it's often difficult to find captive-breds; few young uromastyx are produced in captivity each year, and only a few of the species are bred on a regular basis.

## Advantages of Captive-Bred Uros
Currently, you might be able to find captive-bred young of the Mali uromastyx (*Uromastyx maliensis*), the ornate uro (*U. ornatus*), possibly the Egyptian uro (*U. aegypticus*), and—at high prices—variants of the African uromastyx (*U. acanthinurus*, including several nearly indistinguishable species or subspecies). These species are not bred in large numbers, but they can be found if you spend some time looking for them. Unfortunately, most species are produced by only a few breeders. If a breeder loses interest in the project, a species can virtually disappear from the market until

A hatchling ocellated uro rests calmly in a breeder's hand. Captive-bred uros are more likely to be accustomed to human handling than are wild-caught imports.

another breeder decides to try his or her hand at producing that species.

Captive-bred uros usually are sold when they are a few weeks to a few months old. At this point, they have good colors and body weight for their age, are healthy and feeding on widely available foods, and are not carrying large numbers of intestinal and blood parasites. They probably also know what a human hand is and may enjoy being held and gently petted, rather than scurrying for the hide box when you approach. Captive-breds are of known age, so you won't have to guess when they are old enough for breeding.

### If Only Wild-Caughts are Available

Sometimes you will have to accept wild-collected uromastyx as pets. The number and types of species available as imports vary from time to time, but presently several species are showing up as young specimens (some adults, too) in large numbers. You can usually find wild-caught red-backed (also called rainbow or poreless, *Uromastyx benti*), ocellated (or smooth-eared, *U. ocellatus*), and the Indian uro (*U. hardwicki*) readily and irregularly available as imports; few other species are available, though one never knows what will appear in sporadic shipments from eastern Africa and the Middle East.

Currently, the African uromastyx (*U. acanthinurus* and allies) is protected from exportation in Morocco and a few

Misidentification is a common problem, especially when dealing with imports. One example involves the rainbow uro (*U. benti*). You might find this species listed as *U. benti* (*pseudophilbyi*)—the parenthetical addition meaning "false philbyi"—to distinguish it from *U. philbyi.* The two species are usually discriminated only by the presence of femoral pores in *philbyi*; *benti* lacks them.

other North African countries, so this species seldom is widely available. The entire genus *Uromastyx* is listed by the Convention on International Trade in Endangered Species of Wild Fauna and Flora (CITES) under what is called Appendix II (http://cites.org). CITES is an agreement to attempt to record and to some extent regulate the commercial movement of wild plants and animals across international boundaries in order to prevent them from becoming extinct. The United States and most European countries belong to the organization and comply with its suggestions. An Appendix II listing means, among other things, there is evidence that a species or group of animals (or plants) is facing a threat of local or widespread extermination unless steps are taken to control international trade of the species. Individual countries decide whether to export their lizards and how many can be exported each year; CITES keeps records of these decisions, and the importing countries (mostly the United States and Europe) abide by the wishes of the exporting countries. Thus, if Morocco decides to protect its African uros, the United States will not allow any of these Moroccan lizards into the country. Some countries (such as Togo and Mali) are wide open to exporting their animals, whereas others (such as Ethiopia and the Sudan) virtually never export uros. Countries may change their exportation rules suddenly. This, of course, has a strong effect on which species become available on the market.

If you see a dealer with cages full of young uromastyx, it is wise to question whether they are captive-bred or wild-caught. Because captive-bred specimens can sell at a higher price, some dealers may be tempted to fudge a bit on their specimens' origin. For example, large numbers of young ornate uromastyx recently have appeared on the market with dealers or breeders claiming these uros are captive-bred; actually, they were hatched in African countries from eggs obtained from the wild or from females captive-kept in Africa. Such specimens are better called farmed than captive-bred and can suffer from all the problems (described below) of wild-caught imports.

A reputable breeder will be happy to show you photos of his or her breeding setup and may have the parents to show you as well. Breeders are proud of their accomplishments and generally are happy to share detailed information with you.

## Recognizing a Healthy Uromastyx

Generally, wild-caught uromastyx are problem animals. This doesn't mean they will not survive, just that it will take more persistence on your part to pull them through the acclimation period (sixty to ninety days). They may be highly stressed, skittish, underweight, may not recognize common vegetables as food, and may be carrying literally an army of parasites. Some babies show unhealed umbilical scars on the belly, indicating they were shipped while still absorbing their yolk sacs and probably now have bacterial infections. Such young are extremely delicate and often do not survive more than six weeks even with the best of care—they simply do not adapt to captivity. Even captive-bred young may not be problem free, so be sure to closely inspect every uromastyx before purchasing it. So how do you recognize a uromastyx that is likely to thrive in captivity?

### Eyes

Get an overall impression of the lizard. It should be alert with clear, bright eyes. Any tearing from the eyes may

The fat accumulation under the base of the tail indicates this young female rainbow uro is most likely in good health. A thin or gaunt appearance can signify dehydration or emaciation, and you should avoid purchasing such a specimen.

indicate a respiratory infection, which is common in uromastyx that are kept too cool and not given a hot basking light (see chapter 3).

## Body Weight and Muscle Tone

There should be obvious fat under the base of the tail, indicating that the animal has eaten enough to store some fat. Remember that some uros have folds of loose skin on the sides even when fully fed, so this means little. It's the base of the tail that counts, as well as the strength of the normally thick, strong legs. Check that the toes all are complete, with claws, and that there are no fresh wounds or scars on the body. Commonly, the tip of the tail in imported uros is damaged, but this usually scars over if the animal is kept clean. If older uros are offered for sale, they may show healed scars on the body and neck from breeding fights and encounters with predators; so long as these are not infected, there probably is no harm. Be sure that the jaws are not broken and that the lizard actually can eat.

## Skin

Burns are a common problem with uromastyx because the hot basking light is often not sufficiently protected from contact with the lizards. Burns may be superficial blackish spots (obviously not part of the lizard's pattern) or swollen, infected sores on the back, belly, or feet. Treat all burns, even

minor ones, as major defects and problems—any burn should receive immediate veterinary treatment, and it is best to never purchase a burned uro. (For additional information on lighting and injuries resulting from improper lighting fixtures, see chapters 3 and 6.)

### Feeding

White salt crystals around the nostrils may indicate that the lizard recently was feeding on desert vegetation that contains somewhat toxic chemicals. When you see these crystals, you at least know the uro eats. That's a good sign, though, unfortunately, the uro may not yet recognize vegetables such as peas and kale as acceptable food.

### Activity Level

A uro that just lies about may be ill, or it may be too cool. Few dealers keep their uromastyx warm enough, which may lead to internal problems (such as failure to fully digest food) over a period of just a few days. If the lizard otherwise looks OK and you can get a return guarantee, it still might be worth purchasing, but it's iffy. You want a lizard that looks good and is active. The best uros will actually come up to your hand, out of curiosity, to see what's new in the cage.

In a shop or at an expo, check the general condition of the caging. If the shop keeps its uros in a cage with no basking light or full-spectrum light or has placed the cage near an air-conditioning duct, the lizards likely will become ill. At an expo, dealers sometimes offer their lizards in temporary cages that lack the proper amenities or warmth; these conditions must not last longer than two days. Question dealers to make sure they understand the uro's requirements for proper heating. Also understand that the smaller the specimen, the more likely it is to sicken and die when kept too cool.

## Selecting the Right Species

All the uromastyx available have very similar needs for heating, substrates, and food, so the animal's size is probably the biggest deciding factor for which species to keep. Uros fall into three categories: moderately large, large, and very large. Which type you buy should be determined in part by how much space you have available and your feeding budget. No uro does well in a vivarium less than 3 feet (91 cm) long (width is commonly a third of the vivarium's length), and the largest species prefer a home about 6 feet (183 cm) long. No uro will be comfortable in a 20-gallon (76-liter) aquarium jury-rigged as a vivarium.

The smallest uros we commonly see are moderately large ornate (*Uromastyx ornatus*) and ocellated (*U. ocellatus*) uros, both of which typically mature at only 10 inches (25 cm) long and seldom exceed 12 inches (30 cm). These are among the most colorful species of the genus, are inexpensive when imported, and have a decent survival record. They also are easy to handle and are fairly easy to find. You can keep a single ornate uro in a vivarium about 3 feet (91 cm) long, though it would be more comfortable in a larger home.

In the group of large uros are the African uro (*U. acanthinurus*) and its closely related species and subspecies, including the Mali uro (*U. maliensis*). These heavily built lizards with depressed body types mature at 14 to 16 inches (36 to 41 cm) long. Their colors vary greatly, depending on the area from which they come (which is why it is virtually impossible to put a meaningful specific or subspecific name on all the imports from this species group). As a rule, however, their back is either yellowish to orange red or occasionally dark brown. Some wild females from this species group can be difficult to handle, using the tail and teeth freely; but when purchased as babies, they usually adjust well to handling. Give them a vivarium at least 4 feet (122 cm) long, but bigger if possible.

In the very large category is the cute and cuddly but plainly colored Egyptian uro that typically reaches at least 30 inches (76 cm) in length. Some people claim this lizard grows to 40 inches (1 meter). The Egyptian is a heavy lizard—sometimes more than 4 pounds (1.8 kilos)—with big claws, but even large adults generally enjoy being stroked and will tolerate being picked up. (Careful! Sudden moves may startle your uro, and you could end up with a free-running lizard that damages its legs or jaw and deeply scratches your arms in the process.) To be kept properly, this guy needs room—at least 5 to 6 feet (152 to 183 cm) in length of floor space and a vivarium height of at least 30 inches (76 cm). Though this uro's plain, uniformly dark brown to blackish coloration may make it less attractive than more colorful species, you should weigh this aspect against its great personality.

My suggestion to a beginning uromastyx owner is to find a captive-bred ornate uromastyx, a young specimen that you know is eating and is healthy. Start with a simple vivarium setup at least 3 feet (91 cm) long, and buy the recommended lights and other accessories it will need. As the lizard grows (and it will—quickly), you will gain practical experience in six months that you can use when you move on to a second ornate uro or to a different species. If you must purchase a young wild-caught ornate uromastyx, be sure to have a reptile veterinarian perform a physical exam. At least have the lizard treated for worms and possible blood-borne bacterial infections, or it might die despite veterinary treatment. Avoid any uncommon species at first—those baby Indian uros (*Uromastyx hardwicki*) may be adorable, but the odds are small that a beginner will be able to successfully pull them through their first months. Remember: captive-bred is better!

# CHAPTER 3

# HOUSING

Several days are required to correctly set up the vivarium for a uromastyx, so plan to get all your materials together at least a week before you bring your lizard home. Remember that it could take two or three days to properly adjust the basking lights and position the vivarium where the temperature will drop sufficiently at night. Once acclimated, uromastyx generally are not that difficult to keep—that is, if you consistently give them what they need in terms of temperature, space, and food.

## Caging

Nothing smaller than 3 feet (91 cm) will do for keeping even a small species (such as ornate uros), and you've already been warned that the largest species may need cages 5 to 6 feet (152 to 183 cm) long and 30 inches (76 cm) high. You can use almost any type of cage you wish, as long as it's of the proper size. Common vivaria are made from large glass aquaria (but these are hard to move, break easily, and may

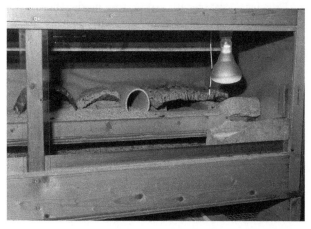

The cork bark and PVC pipe shelters and the horizontal shelf in this home-made wooden enclosure create several hiding areas.

crack under the hot basking lights), wooden or fiberglass commercial cages, and molded rubber or galvanized metal stock tubs designed as water tubs for cattle and horses (often an economical choice). Because of the size of the vivarium, as well as the need to hang the lights over it, some keepers prefer metal or molded rubber tubs, which can be placed on a sturdy metal frame or just left on the floor. You can't see through the sides of the tubs, but they are very durable, easy to handle, and less likely to break than are aquaria.

You may want to keep the vivarium as simple as possible. Your pet will not need plants in its cage—not even plastic plants—and the only decorations you need are a hide box, a basking stone, perhaps a climbing perch, and a food dish (no water dish—see the following discussion on humidity).

## Temperature and Lighting

All uromastyx species come from hot, dry climates. Some (such as the African uro) are at home on the edges of the Sahara desert in northern Africa, whereas others are found as isolated relics of cooler, wetter times in the Arabian Desert. Even the species from relatively moderate habitats still burrow into hard, dry ground in the shade of sparse bushes, and they spend part of the morning basking on rocks. All are terrestrial burrowers adapted to hot daytime temperatures and the coolness of the desert nights. For your pets to thrive in the vivarium, you must simulate these conditions.

Uros have very specific temperature needs. Their home must be kept at an ambient (overall) temperature of roughly 80°F to 90°F (26.5°C to 32°C) for ten to fourteen hours a day. There must be a hot (*hot*, not warm) basking spot that allows the lizard to reach a core body temperature of as much as 120°F (49°C) when it chooses to bask during the day (usually in the morning and late afternoon). All heat must be supplied from above, because undertank heating (such as heating pads and strips) will prevent the lizard from being able to dig down to a cooler area in the vivarium when it wishes. In the evening, the temperature in the vivarium must be allowed to drop sharply to about 65°F (18°C) until the next morning. These are pretty stringent requirements, but they really aren't hard to meet with the equipment we have today.

## Basking Lights

As you might expect of a large lizard that basks several hours a day, uromastyx need access to either natural sunlight that is not filtered through window glass (which removes the important ultraviolet components of the light) or artificial lights that simulate sunlight. Few hobbyists can manage to move their uro vivaria into the sunlight each day (being careful that the uro does not overheat and making sure it can get into the shade if it desires), though some do place tubs on a frame with wheels to ease relocation. Most hobbyists prefer to use full-spectrum lights—specially coated fluorescent tubes that provide a significant amount of ultraviolet A and ultraviolet B light. The UV-B light is essential because it allows the lizard to convert chemicals in the blood into vitamin $D_3$, which in turn controls metabolism and deposition of calcium in the bones and the rest of the body. Without UV-B light and vitamin $D_3$, a source of calcium, no uro can thrive—and young uros will quickly die.

The usual lighting arrangement is two 4-foot (122-cm) full-spectrum fluorescent tubes producing 5 percent to 7 percent UV-B (carefully read the label on the tube) placed in a simple fixture available at pet-supply stores. Mount the fixture on the screen lid of the vivarium for support. The

Clip-on lamps are readily available at pet-supply stores and serve well as basking lights. Their metal domes concentrate the heat, which helps prevent heat loss to the sides.

UV-B light does not penetrate very far, so the tubes should be as close to the lizard as possible—30 inches (76 cm) or less, never farther away than that. In deep vivaria, provide the lizard with a raised platform that allows it to get closer to the light. Replace full-spectrum tubes every six months to a year because they lose efficiency.

### Preventing Burns

Even though fluorescent lights run at cool temperatures, make sure they are always above a screened top and out of reach of the lizard to prevent burns.

Recently, mercury vapor lamps that produce both high basking temperatures and a decent amount of UV-B light have become available, though they still are expensive. UV-B from a mercury vapor lamp penetrates farther than does UV-B from a fluorescent tube, so mercury vapor lamps may be preferred for use in very large and tall vivaria. These lamps become very warm, however, and you may need a small fan to prevent the lamps from overheating.

When properly used, basking lights will also control the ambient temperature. Every vivarium must have at least one (preferably two or three in larger vivaria) incandescent light hung over it in a metal dome to concentrate the heat. The light(s) should cover just half the cage so as to leave a shaded, cooler retreat area. By using bulbs of 100 to 125 watts and varying their distance above the vivarium, you can easily control the final temperature on a flat basking rock so the basking site reaches the necessary 120°F to 140°F (49°C to 60°C). In addition to providing concentrated heat to the basking site, these lights heat the substrate and the air in the vivarium to roughly 80°F (26.5°C) in the coolest corner away from the lights. This temperature range is referred to as the thermal gradient and gives the lizard the ability to thermoregulate (to control its body temperature by relocating to a warmer or cooler spot as desired) throughout the day. When the basking lights are turned off in early evening, the temperature of the vivarium will quickly drop to that of your reptile room;

keep your uro in a room that is kept cool at night, prefer-ably air-conditioned and maintained at about 65°F (18°C).

Regular household incandescent bulbs will work for the basking lights, but special basking bulbs and spotlights with silvered globes are more efficient as they waste less heat to the sides and thus are a bit cheaper to run. Or you can use mercury vapor lights, which produce high temperatures at a rapid rate. Your pet shop will have a variety of bulbs that work for uros. At the same time you are looking at lights, look for a heavy-duty timer that will automatically and safely switch the lights on and off at intervals—for example, at 8 a.m. and 8 p.m. for a twelve-hour day.

Remember that the lizard must be completely unable to reach the basking light and its dome. Typically, basking lights are hung from a wooden bar suspended above the vivarium; this also helps prevent melting of rubber stock tubs and uneven heating and eventual breaking of glass aquaria. Use a screen lid from the pet store or make one with quarter-inch (6-millimeter) hardware cloth on a wooden frame as an extra precaution to ensure that larger uromastyx cannot climb out and burn themselves on the light. Never place the basking light over the center of the vivarium, as this will destroy the temperature gradient.

## Thermometers

Use at least one but preferably two thermometers in the vivarium to be sure you know the true temperatures at the hottest and coolest ends. Don't guess! Monitor the tempera-ture under the basking light (up to 140°F, 60°C) and also under the hide box (80°F, 26.5°C) at the cool end. Simple and inexpensive electronic thermometers with sensors at the end of long cords are widely available at pet-supply stores and even electronic stores. The best styles come with built-in hygrometers to measure relative humidity in the vivarium in addition to temperature.

## Humidity

As you might expect of desert lizards, uromastyx are uncomfortable with high relative humidities and prefer dry air. Aim for a maximum humidity of 70 percent during the evening and 50 percent during the day under the hide box; lower levels generally are better. Do not place a water dish in the vivarium—uros seldom drink, and spilled water will quickly raise the humidity. In the United States, a room with air-conditioning or central heating (both of which dehumidify the air) may be necessary to drop the humidity to suitable levels; a dehumidifier also may work. Use a hygrometer to measure the humidity in the vivarium—there is no way for you to accurately guess humidity levels.

Humidity is an important factor if you plan to keep your pet outdoors during the hottest days of summer. In much of the eastern and southern United States, the summer humidity commonly reaches 80 percent or more for days on end, which could be devastating to a uromastyx. The exposure to natural sunlight may be good for a uro, but high humidity can be a killer.

## Substrate

Keep the substrate simple and inexpensive. Sand works well because it has relatively rounded grains; it is washed by the manufacturer and is available from pet-supply stores. Avoid sharp, dirty construction sand, which might contain contaminants. You can try other substrates, such as small pebbles, but sand works best. If you worry about the lizard accidentally ingesting sand—which can lead to gut impaction (intestinal blockage)—remember that these lizards feed naturally in sand and accidents certainly are rare. Put some newspaper under the food dish if you are a real worrywart. Keep the substrate clean by removing feces and old food at least daily.

Put at least 6 inches (15 cm) of sand in the vivarium to allow the lizard to dig a bit. This is sufficient for digging in a vivarium; if you were to let a lizard burrow as it would in nature, you'd need to provide at least 3 or 4 feet (91 or 122 cm) of substrate.

Baby uros are best kept on newspaper. You need to keep a close eye on your baby uro's droppings to make sure it is digesting properly; this requires changing the substrate at

Terra cotta and rock slabs can serve as simple shelters.

least daily. Paper is inexpensive and simple to replace, and you don't have to worry as much about gut impaction as you would with sand.

## Hide Boxes

Every uro needs a hide box. If you are keeping two uromastyx in one large vivarium (which is not recommended), each needs its own box. Use a plastic box of the appropriate size (about 6 inches, 15 cm, high and two-thirds the length of the lizard—remember it will curl in the box and likes a tight fit) with a hole cut in one or two sides for easy access and egress. The hide box should be somewhat more humid than the rest of the terrarium, so consider a substrate of half sand and half vermiculite that is kept barely moist. If you notice the lizard avoiding the box, it's probably too moist, so let the vermiculite dry out.

If you want to fancy up the enclosure a bit, add one or two patio blocks—flat concrete building blocks that usually have one or two holes through their middles. Place them near the basking area, where the uro will use them as if they were natural caves.

# CHAPTER 4

# FEEDING

O ver the past decade, keepers have come to believe that adult uromastyx are almost strictly vegetarians, seldom eating insects that pass through their habitat. This would make sense when you consider that their intestines are structured into pouches that allow the bacterial fermentation of tough cellulose into digestible starches and sugars. Observations in nature indicate that adult uros feed on a wide variety of often harsh, "chemically empowered" shrubs that are toxic to other lizards; and they also take many softer greens, as well as a variety of seeds that they crush with their strong, fused molars. Babies and juveniles, however, are not strictly vegetarian; they take a less restrictive diet that includes some beetles, flies, and other insects. Fortunately, it is fairly easy to feed captive uros.

## Salads and Seeds

The mainstay of the uromastyx diet, at all ages, is a good green salad consisting of chopped or shredded collard and turnip greens, endive, bright green and red romaine lettuces, mustard greens, and dandelion greens in season. These items should be offered after washing or misting, as the greens themselves and the water on them are the major source of water for most uros. Supplement greens with a variety of vegetables such as shredded carrots and fresh, frozen and thawed, or canned (with salty fluids rinsed off) corn, green peas, zucchini and other squash, and shredded green beans. To cover the seed-eating propensities of uromastyx, offer small amounts of white millet, safflower, and clover seeds, and even a few sesame seeds. Generally, avoid sunflower seeds because of their high fat content.

Many keepers offer their adult uromastyx a few dry beans in every meal. These can include such favorites as lima beans, navy beans, white beans, pinto beans, and field peas. Baby uros need to have these food items finely chopped or ground into particles that are small enough to chew and swallow.

As a rule, avoid the cabbage vegetables such as broccoli and brussels sprouts, which may interfere with calcium intake (though napa, or Chinese, cabbage is a great source of calcium and seldom causes digestive problems). The same is said of spinach, but a small amount seldom hurts—uros take much more chemically active plants in nature.

Adding a good grade of calcium supplement to the salad certainly won't hurt baby uromastyx, which are growing fast and using lots of calcium in their bones. Adults need less supplementation. If you give calcium supplements (either as powders from the reptile section of the pet shop or as chunked or ground cuttlebone from the bird department), be sure to add small amounts of vitamin $D_3$ supplement as well. Never add large amounts of any supplement to the diet; calcium and vitamin overdoses are possible even in baby uros.

Your local pet store should carry seed mixes and commercially prepared pellet food suitable for uromastyx.

Make sure the size of the food matches the size of the uro's mouth. Obviously, baby uros need considerably smaller pieces of food than what large adults can handle. Green peas can be chopped or smashed into a pulp for babies, and zucchini and green beans chopped into bits of less than a quarter-inch (6-mm).

## Insects

Though adult uromastyx can be treated as strict vegetarians much as green iguanas (*Iguana iguana*) are, growing baby uromastyx seem to need a somewhat higher protein diet to grow well. Once a week, you can offer two or three crickets or mealworms or even chopped superworms. Dust the insects with calcium supplements and, if possible, feed the bugs a gut-loading food mix (available at the pet shop) before you offer them to the uro. Your uro will chase down and devour adult mealworm beetles. Don't overdo insects, especially with adults (though it seems likely that uros in nature are a bit more omnivorous than many keepers like to believe).

## Feeding Frequency

Feed baby uros once a day; morning is best so the food is properly digested after they have basked and warmed up their bodies. Feed adults every other day—they may become obese if fed too often. Remove old food by the early afternoon on

The domestic brown cricket is a good source of protein for growing baby uromastyx.

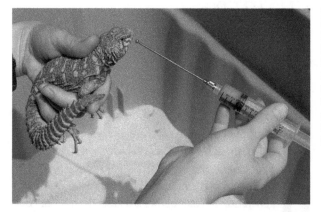

the day it is offered; this prevents the lizard from eating too late in the day and gives it a chance to at least partially digest its food before the temperature drops at night.

Offer food in shallow pottery bowls; these hold the slightly damp salad and keep it from mixing with the sand substrate. You can place the bowls on newspaper if you worry about sand ingestion. Insects can be allowed to run free to provide some exercise for the uromastyx.

## Water

Adult uromastyx seldom or never drink from open water, and it should not be in their vivarium. Baby uros, however, need more water than adults do; once a week, place them for a few minutes in a shallow bowl of fresh water to hydrate them by drinking and also letting some water soak into their skin between the scales. Or, better yet, you can offer them water from an eye dropper. Holding your baby uro and offering it water by the drop is a good bonding experience. As mentioned above, lightly misting salads with water before you feed them to your uro adds to the water they already receive from the greens themselves. Newly imported uromastyx do need more water than established pets do; we'll discuss that in chapter 6.

# CHAPTER 5

# BREEDING

U nfortunately, uromastyx are not especially easy to breed, though some keepers have been able to maintain *Uromastyx ornatus, U. acanthinurus,* and *U. aegypticus* in the home through at least three or four generations. What follows is a basic "recipe" for cooling and breeding; each species may have some differences, and not all keepers succeed even when they do everything correctly. It may be a matter of having perfectly compatible uros in the best of health or just being lucky. Be patient and you most likely will succeed.

## Sexes

It seems that most uromastyx take at least two, and probably three, years to become sexually mature. This applies to both large and small species. If you attempt to breed lizards that are less than the full adult size for their species and are not showing distinct sexual characteristics, you probably will not succeed. Uros are not easy to sex—though, as a rule, male uromastyx have somewhat heavier heads with larger jowls than females do, even in small species. Behavior is not much help either, as in some species (Mali uromastyx, for instance) females are more aggressive than males and may control premating and postmating behavior. In some species, especially ornate and ocellated uros, males are much more brightly colored than females are and may display colors, such as green and blue, that are not developed in females.

All uros except the red-backed uromastyx (*Uromastyx benti*) and the armored uromastyx (*U. princeps*) have pores under the femora of the hind legs (femoral pores) and across the area above the vent (preanal pores). The pores are not simple holes or pimples in the scales; they are

Male Saharan uromastyx display brighter ventral coloring than do females as shown with this side-by-side comparison of a female (left) and a male (right).

each surrounded by a ring of tiny scales. Pores are found in both sexes and all ages, so they are generally not useful for distinguishing sexes. In some species, such as African uromastyx, the pores are about the same size and development in adults of both sexes and are worthless for sexing.

However, in other species, such as ornate uros and Egyptian uros, sexually mature males exude a brown, waxy substance from their femoral and preanal pores. This substance, which a male uses to mark a territory and tell a female that he is present, often adheres to the pores and sticks out like short, brown, comb teeth. If you see this, you can be pretty sure you have a male. Males of these species have larger and better-developed pores than females.

Male uromastyx have short hemipenes at the base of the tail that sometimes produce a widened tail base or a pouched look, whereas females have a narrower base. This distinction may be hard to see. So far, sexing with a sexing probe has not proved useful in distinguishing uromastyx sexes.

Male (left) Mali uros have generally stronger ventral pigment and larger femoral pores than females (right) have.

## Natural Cycles

Uromastyx breeders have found that a fairly routine cooling period leads to successful mating. Since many desert areas have cold winters, this may be a practical simulation of natural cycles, though little is known of how most uromastyx prepare for breeding in nature. It is known that a cool period allows the cells that produce the sperm to mature in many other lizards, and this probably happens in uromastyx as well. Certainly, it seems that the mating urge is strong when the lizards come out of the cooling period.

Cooling uromastyx is not difficult. Before cooling, all lizards should be mature and very healthy, with some fat at the base of the tail and no signs of respiratory or parasite problems. House each lizard separately, and start tapering off the food about a week before cooling. Over the same period, gradually lower the basking temperature to 100°F (38°C) and reduce the number of hours allowed for basking. The lizards must be allowed to finish digesting all food in their gut before being cooled, which the slow reduction of basking temperatures will ensure. At the same time, reduce the length of daylight to about eight hours a day. The ambient temperatures should remain close to 80°F (26.5°C) during the day and 65°F (18°C) at night.

Now you are ready to cool your uromastyx. Turn off the basking lights one evening and let the cage temperature drop to 65°F (18°C) as usual for the night. Hold the cage and the lizard at this low temperature for two to three months (yes, eight to twelve weeks) without feeding. Once a week you can give the lizard some water, either from a dropper or by placing the uro in a shallow bowl of water for a few minutes. The uro should stay in the security of its hide box during this period, though it may occasionally come out and move sluggishly about. You can leave the fluorescent tubes on for eight hours a day so the uro maintains a sense of passing time. To be on the safe side, you can turn on a weak basking light (producing perhaps 80°F, 26.5°C) for four hours a day, two or three times a week. This probably simulates, to some extent, natural conditions, as these lizards do not go into a deep sleep during their cooling period (technically called the brumation period) and will come out during warm periods.

After the cooling period is over, bring the lizard back up to normal daytime temperatures under hot basking lights over about a week's time. You may want to rehydrate the uro by placing it in a bowl of shallow water once a day for four or five days, never for more than a few minutes. The uromastyx should pass any feces that developed in its lower intestine over the brumation period and probably also will go through a complete piecemeal shed (typically, the skin

Breeding success is largely credited to following a cooling routine, which some hobbyists say simulates natural winter cycles in the desert. The cooling period usually begins in December and ends in early March—mating is probable when the lizards are brought up to normal temperatures.

would be shed in large chunks that are torn off and eaten by the lizard over just a few days). It also should be very hungry and will start eating again. After one to two weeks, everything should be back to normal.

## Basic Breeding Routines

To take advantage of naturally low temperatures, uromastyx generally are cooled during the late autumn and winter months and then bred in early spring. Start the cooling period at the beginning of December, and hold the lizards in a cool area until late February or the first week of March. Bring them back to normal keeping conditions as suggested above, and make sure they are feeding and defecating. This is a good time to worm the female just to make sure she will not pass worm eggs on to her young. Allow the lizards a full month to regain lost weight and assume normal behaviors and activity levels.

In April, place the lizards together in a large vivarium— at least 4 feet (122 cm) long for ornate uromastyx, larger for the bigger species. The male (generally) marks off a territory by rubbing scent substances over a central rock or patio stone, and he may flatten the sand in the area by turning in tight circles. He quickly detects the presence of the female and grasps her by the nape using his mouth. Then he turns her over (assuming she is ready to mate and does not

The white markings on this female Egyptian uro are from a male making a territorial display. Males may also mark submissive males and claim their territory by leaving these scent marks on basking rocks or shelters.

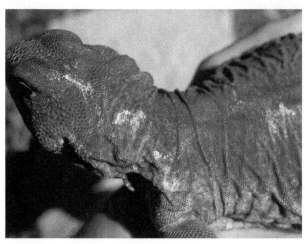

escape), slides his vent over hers, and places a hemipenis in her vent to inseminate her. At this point, the lizards separate and go their own way. If you keep a compatible pair together for a few weeks, expect several matings and an increased chance of fertile eggs.

In some species, such as the African uromastyx, the female may strongly reject the male's attention, and fighting could occur. Two uros fighting can lead to serious bite wounds and lost toes or even legs, so pay close attention to the actions of your lizards when they are put together, during and after mating. Separating the lizards after one mating may be the safest course.

The female's vivarium should include a deep nest box containing sand and moist vermiculite. She usually lays her eggs in a nest hole dug in the bottom of the nest box. The nest is made about a month after mating and may contain eight to twenty-five eggs, depending in part on the size of the species and individual. The eggs are 1 to 1.5 inches (2.5 to 3.8 cm) long, oval, and whitish. They should be removed to an incubator and kept on slightly moist vermiculite (at most 60 to 70 percent humidity) for about three months at 85°F to 90°F (26.5°C to 32°C). Many eggs will not hatch, and entire clutches may disintegrate from not being fertile or for unknown reasons. Successful mating does not necessarily lead to successful hatching.

A female ornate uro flips upside down to show she is unwilling to mate.

The young—if you are fortunate enough to get some—are about 3 inches (7.6 cm) long. They look much like the adults but have short heads with big eyes and usually have somewhat different color patterns, emphasizing brown and yellowish crossbands or spots. Relocate them to their own vivaria as soon as possible and raise them individually to prevent fighting and to better control their feeding and health. Provide them with food of the proper size (chopped salad mixings and a few insects that the baby uro can easily take into its mouth) and water from a shallow bowl or a dropper. Newspaper is the best substrate. Baby uros do not need excessively warm basking temperatures for the first year; they are able to digest their food at just 100°F to 120°F (38°C to 49°C). Expect the babies to nearly double in length every three or four months over the first year.

## The Easiest Breeders

Currently, only four of the generally accepted fifteen species of uromastyx have been consistently bred in captivity. This just means that several breeders have produced two or more clutches of eggs that hatched and produced living young, not that these species can be bred on demand every year. These are, of course, the species that are most likely to be sold as captive-bred young.

Perhaps the most widely bred uro today is the ornate uromastyx, which has been bred by several people since the

Bulging with eggs, this gravid ocellated uro will soon lay her clutch. Laying occurs about one month after mating.

Ocellated baby uros break through their shells.

early 1990s. There also has been limited success with ocellated uromastyx, a close relative of the ornate. Red-backed or poreless uromastyx are rumored to be bred in captivity, but almost all those offered as captive-bred are actually farmed in Africa.

Also widely seen at the moment are captive-bred Mali uromastyx. This species is closely related to the African uromastyx, which has a reputation for being a difficult and inconsistent breeder (though German hobbyists have bred African uros for decades). Being bred with some frequency is the large Egyptian uromastyx, which may have been the first species to be bred consistently in both Germany and the United States.

# CHAPTER 6

# HEALTH MAINTENANCE

O nce acclimated to the vivarium, uromastyx are hardy lizards that commonly live ten to twenty years. However, they are more subject to parasite infestations and to death from problems in the vivarium than most lizards are.

## Environmental Problems

Most deaths of uromastyx occur within two weeks to six months of purchase, as the lizards attempt to adapt to vivarium conditions. Part of this is due to preexisting health problems in imported wild-caught specimens, and part is due to hobbyists' misunderstanding of the lizards' needs for living in the vivarium.

## Hydration

Many imported uromastyx are dehydrated. Unfortunately, they have been shipped long distances, crowded perhaps dozens to a container, fed little or no suitable food, and given water only by misting. This eventually can cause the

Mali hatchlings nibble on a hibiscus bloom—a favorite food. Uromastyx do not typically drink water from a bowl. They receive the water they need from the food they eat.

kidneys of young specimens and even adults to fail, and it may be impossible to rescue a uro that has been poorly kept for several weeks. If you purchase a wild-caught uromastyx, rehydrate it as soon as possible. This consists of simply placing the specimen in a shallow dish of warm water twice a day and allowing it to drink (although drinking water is uncommon among uros, it may happen with young specimens and some gravid females). If the uro doesn't drink, leave it in the water dish a few minutes to let some water soak into the skin between the scales. Don't expect the lizard to start lapping water like a dog (though this can happen); it is more likely to just get its jaws and belly wet. Dry the uro off before putting it back into the vivarium.

Be sure that all greens offered to new specimens have been washed or at least misted so there are drops of water adhering to the leaves. This is how uromastyx get most of their water in nature, and it should be sufficient for vivarium specimens once they acclimate.

Expect any wild-caught uromastyx to take at least two weeks, sometimes a month in the case of older adults, to adjust to the vivarium. This is the period when most deaths occur.

## Wrong Temperature and Humidity

Too low a temperature will lead to reduced feeding, inability to digest the food, and a lingering death. You must provide a suitable basking area that is kept hot for at least four hours in the morning and four hours in the afternoon, when the lizard is most likely to bask for long periods. The basking spots must be at least 100°F (38°C), with at least part of the area reaching between 120°F and 140°F (49°C and 60°C). Lower basking temperatures will not suffice, and neither can the lowest daytime temperature drop much lower than 80°F (26.5°C). These temperatures assure that the uromastyx can attain and hold a core body temperature that allows it to digest its food. (See also the Temperature section in chapter 3.)

High humidity leads to a lingering death in uros that is hard to detect. Keep an eye on your uromastyx. If the lizard is sluggish, has developed skin problems, and eats poorly, it may be slowly dying. If kept at a daytime humidity of much higher than 60 percent, your uromastyx will not thrive and probably will die within six months.

## Lighting Problems

A young uromastyx that is not given access to sufficient UV-B light will develop rickets and other weak-bone problems, soft jaws, and swollen legs—all signs of what commonly is called metabolic bone disease. This will happen even if you load the food with calcium and vitamin $D_3$ supplements. Assuming you cannot give your pet access to unfiltered sunlight for several hours a day so it can bask, you must supply UV-B light with the proper full-spectrum fluorescent tubes or with mercury vapor lights. Note: There is no substitute for these two light sources, including plant lights and black lights (some people mistakenly believe these to be adequate UV-B light sources). (See also chapter 3.)

## Parasites

Captive-bred uromastyx seldom come with heavy parasite loads, but this certainly is not true of imports, which should always be wormed and carefully checked for mites. A full veterinary examination is best but seldom is given to uromastyx because of the cost.

## Worms

A real problem with many uros imported directly from Africa (including those that are farmed) is that they carry tremendous loads of nematode worms (roundworms) in the gut. Though some of these worms seem to function in digestion of the food, many are harmful parasites. All newly purchased imported uros must be wormed as soon as possible, preferably after a veterinary examination for other problems.

Worming can be done at home by an experienced lizard keeper, though it is considered potentially dangerous and life-threatening for your lizard. Your veterinarian is better suited for safely dosing these lizards than you are. For adult uromastyx, which are relatively large and heavy lizards, it is common practice to add a pinch (such as can be taken with the tips of a pair of tweezers) of fenbendazole (Panacur) to the food to treat for nematodes. The recommended first dose is about 100 milligrams per kilogram (per 2.2 pounds) of lizard. In two weeks, this dose is followed by a second dose. The treatment will kill some of the helpful worm fauna of the lizard's gut, so adding droppings from healthy uros (already wormed) to the food of the uro undergoing treatment helps replenish the good nematodes.

## Bacteria

There are several reports of imported uros suffering from blood-borne bacterial and protozoal infections. These infections usually require veterinary treatment to combat them. You can't just dose uromastyx with broad-spectrum antibiotics because these kill the good bacteria in the gut as well as the harmful ones in the blood. Gut bacteria are essential for fermentation of the food; if these bacteria all die, the uro also will die, even if it continues eating. If your vet recommends using an antibiotic, try giving the lizard a lactobacillus compound (available in the pet shop) or even a small amount of yogurt with active cultures to reestablish a good bacterial flora in the gut.

## Mites and Ticks

These arachnid pests feed on small blood vessels in the skin and often attach around the eyes, the ears, and the vent, as well as under the toes. Ticks are large mites (often more than a quarter-inch, 6 mm, long) that anchor in place with their spiny mouthparts and can be gently pulled out when detected. Put a small dab of antibiotic ointment on the attachment spot to prevent infections if the tick's mouthparts stay in the skin. Ticks almost never reproduce in the vivarium and are not a problem with captive-bred uros.

Small translucent yellowish or brownish mites that become red when filled with blood are a more serious problem. These lizard mites can be transferred among almost all types of lizards in the pet shop or home and can weaken a

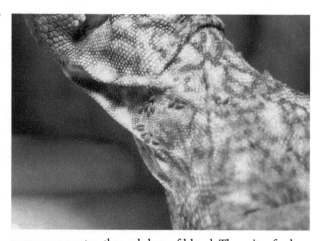

Wedged into the neck folds of this imported Somali uro is a cluster of mites. Parasites are common in imported specimens. Thoroughly check any lizard considered for purchase as mites may be hidden in whorls of the tail or in skin folds under the uro's legs or near its neck or vent areas.

young uromastyx through loss of blood. The mites feed on the lizard at night, spending the day in cracks in the vivarium frame and in the decorations and lay their eggs. Most wild-caught uromastyx have a few mites around the eyes and ears. These can be treated by wiping down the lizard with a cloth dampened in olive oil, which suffocates the mites. Pet shops also sell safe miticides that can be used on even small uromastyx with few losses (miticides have a reputation for occasionally causing deaths of small and young lizards). The problem is that the eggs hatch in a week and you have another generation of mites attacking the lizard. This means you must not only kill the mites on the uro but also sanitize the vivarium to kill the eggs—or you can repeat the mite treatment at weekly intervals (at least three times) to kill all newly hatched mites.

## Common Accidents

Even a uromastyx kept by itself in an enclosure can have accidents. If you keep a close eye on your lizard and make the vivarium as safe as possible, your pet seldom should need first aid.

### Burns

Obviously, hanging a hot basking light over a vivarium in a metal dome creates a serious burn hazard. If you've ever touched a hot basking-light dome with your hand while opening or closing a vivarium cover, you know how quickly your skin will burn. In the case of uromastyx, most of their temperature-sensing mechanisms are in the upper surface of their skin, where they can sense the heat from sunlight while basking. If a uromastyx comes into contact with a basking light and grasps it with its legs, it might just hang on until the leg is burned through without detecting a problem. This is why you sometimes see uros for sale that are severely burned. In addition, a hot rock type of heater that malfunctions can severely burn the lizard's belly and tail, where it can't detect dangerous temperatures.

A lizard's minor burns are treated much as human burns are. Keep the wound very clean and lubricate it with a burn ointment from your veterinarian. Don't cover the wound—burns heal best when exposed to the air. However, burns easily become infected, so apply topical antibiotics to the wound until new skin grows in completely, which can take several weeks. If the burn penetrates deeply into the muscles or into the body cavity, your veterinarian probably will suggest euthanasia because treatment will be difficult or impossible.

## Caution

Keep all lights out of the uromastyx's reach!

### Bites

Uromastyx are aggressive lizards that usually don't like the company of others of their kind. Put two uros together in a fairly small vivarium, and they will fight. This is true even when they are babies. The teeth of uromastyx can crush seeds, and they can produce ripping, jagged cuts. Not uncommonly, two uros will battle until one dies (especially when babies). Even in casual encounters, a uromastyx may pull off another's toe. Bites also commonly result from fights during courtship and mating. If a uromastyx loses a toe in a fight, the stump usually heals quickly and scars with no major loss of function for the leg. Minor bites (those that barely break the skin) seldom present a problem, as similar wounds must occur in nature (many imported uromastyx

An Egyptian uro in mid-shed shows patches of discoloration where the old skin meets the new skin.

are scarred). If kept clean and checked for infection, they will quickly heal.

Deep wounds may require suturing by a veterinarian and will likely become infected. Though infections are easily treated with both oral and topical broad-spectrum antibiotics, remember that these same antibiotics kill the gut bacteria of the uro, interfering with digestion. So, use antibiotics sparingly. If you think your uro has a digestion problem, be sure the veterinarian understands that uros are not typical lizards; you may have to use a lactobacillus mixture to replace the gut flora after antibiotic treatment.

## Shedding

Like most other lizards, uros shed several times a year, but the skin comes off in large and small pieces rather than a single piece as in snakes. The uro may rub different parts of its body to start the skin peeling off and use its jaws to pull off the pieces, often eating the old skin in the process. As long as the pieces don't stay on the body for days on end, there is no problem. You may never notice your uro molting other than some dull areas on the back or sides. If you think your uro has a molting problem, don't soak it as you would many other lizards. Instead, try to gently rub off adhering skin with a wet cotton ball, massaging a bit of water into the skin in the trouble area.

# CHAPTER 7

# POPULAR UROMASTYX SPECIES

Currently, some fifteen species of uromastyx are recognized, but not all are well-defined. Some probably are synonyms or subspecies of other species, and a few are so rare they have seldom been studied by herpetologists. If you are patient and keep checking dealer lists on the Internet, as well as frequent reptile expos and shops throughout the country, you probably can find representatives of four common and at least three uncommon species. Identification of uncommon species may be difficult or nearly impossible without technical literature and preserved specimens for comparison.

## Species Groups
The fifteen species of uromastyx generally are thought to represent six groups of closely related species and subspecies. As a rule, the species of a group are similar in appearance and in how they are kept in the vivarium. The following are the currently recognized species of the genus *Uromastyx* arranged by species groups, with a few comments on range, identification, and availability.

## Acanthinurus Group
Included here are the African uromastyx (*Uromastyx acanthinurus*) and its allies. In these large (usually more than 14 inches, 36 cm), heavy-tailed, and depressed-body species, the scales on the back are small but distinct (about 130 in number down the center of the back), and the large scales under the tail form distinct rows like those on top of the tail.

Species limits in this group are difficult to distinguish, and there is no general agreement on the valid species. Currently, hobbyists recognize the Mali uro (*U. maliensis*) from the extreme southwestern edge of the group's range as valid, though almost impossible to distinguish from some African uromastyx. The taxa known as *U. geyri* (the Saharan uro from the Algeria-Niger border area) and *U. dispar* (upper Sudan) are questionably distinct from the African uro and may be at best subspecies. All these species occur in the western Sahara desert and vicinity.

### Aegypticus Group

The single species usually recognized here is very similar to the Acanthinurus group, but even larger, with tiny scales and wrinkled skin on the sides. This is the Egyptian uromastyx (*Uromastyx aegypticus*) found from Iran to Egypt.

### Princeps Group

Virtually unknown to hobbyists or scientists, two rare species are placed here. Both have very short, wide tails that are less than half the length of the head and body and strongly armored with spines. The armored uromastyx (*Uromastyx princeps*) lacks femoral and preanal pores and comes from the deserts of Somalia. The Omani uromastyx (*U. thomasi*) sports a rather disk-shaped tail with shorter spines and comes from southeastern Arabia.

African (Moroccan) uros such the adult male shown here are typically are a bit more aggressive than other uro species. However, regular handling can to some extent tame these large lizards.

This dwarf ocellated uro displays a sharp pattern down its back.

## Ornatus Group

There are at least five closely related species or subspecies in this group of relatively small uros. They usually have a spotted pattern, and the scales under the tip of the tail are fused into large scales rather than rings (as they are on top of the tail). Included here is the familiar ornate uromastyx (*Uromastyx ornatus*), as well as the look-alike ocellated uro (*U. ocellatus*) that lacks a row of spiny scales at the front of the ear opening. Ornate uros come from northeastern Egypt and the Sinai Desert, whereas ocellated uros are from southern Egypt and Sudan. The red-backed or poreless uromastyx (*U. benti*) from Yemen lacks femoral and preanal pores. Almost unknown to hobbyists are Yemeni uromastyx (*U. philbyi*) from north Yemen and Somali uromastyx (*U. macfadyeni*); both may be subspecies of the ornate uromastyx.

## Asmussi Group

The two species of this group are never seen by hobbyists and are almost unknown in life, seldom having been observed even by herpetologists. Both come from the deserts of Iraq to Pakistan and have two or more rows of small, regular scales between the enlarged spiny scales on top of the tail. Some have large, red spines on the back. These uros have fewer rows of spines on the tail than does

Look at the tail spikes on this Indian uro. The spikes are much smaller in *U. hardwicki* than in other uro species.

the related Indian uromastyx. *Uromastyx asmussi* is known as the Iranian uromastyx, whereas the very similar *U. loricatus* is the Iraqi uro.

### Hardwicki Group

Once offered in fair numbers, the Indian uromastyx (*Uromastyx hardwicki*) now is only sporadically seen, usually as babies that seldom survive more than a few weeks. This large species (18 inches, 46 cm) is found in rocky plains and near-deserts from Afghanistan into northwestern India and is more colonial than other uromastyx. There are at least thirty-four rows of spiny scales on the tail, these further separated by rows of smaller scales. Adults tend to be brownish with traces of darker spots. Just a few breeders have had limited success producing this species in captivity, so captive-breds are hard to find.

## Available Species

Not all the uromastyx species are generally available, and several (such as *Uromastyx princeps*) have never been kept by hobbyists. The following are the most familiar species, those likely to be found by a determined hobbyist at pet shops, reptile expos, and through mail order dealers.

## African Uromastyx

*Uromastyx acanthinurus* long has been a favorite lizard of European keepers, with specimens imported from Morocco and Algeria in northwestern Africa; it often has been called the Moroccan uromastyx. This is a large lizard, often more than 16 inches (41 cm) long, with a heavy tail, depressed form, and especially sturdy legs. Most specimens are shades of brown with a paler spotted or netted pattern, but some may be shades of yellow or even orange when warm and fully acclimated to the vivarium. The scales of the back are small but large enough to be countable, and the skin of the sides is smooth and not strongly wrinkled. The snout is distinctly pointed in most specimens. Sexes may be almost impossible to distinguish in this species, though females often are more aggressive than males.

Currently, Morocco protects this species and does not allow legal exports, so those that appear come from neighboring countries, are long-term captives, or are illegally imported. Unless you are sure your specimen has been captive-bred (this species has a poor breeding record), it must be treated for parasites.

This African uro displays a nuchal (neck) marking.

## Mali Uromastyx

First identified in 1996, *Uromastyx maliensis* comes from hard-packed sandy deserts in Mali at the southwestern edge of the Sahara desert region. Here, the species is a burrower

in a harsh habitat with few shrubs or grasses. Adults commonly are 14 inches (36 cm) long or longer, with the male carrying brighter colors on the back when warm and healthy and kept under the proper temperature and humidity conditions. One mark of this species is that the yellow back contrasts strongly with the black legs and head (though this pattern is seen on occasion in the African uromastyx as well). Imported in considerable numbers from Mali since 1995, this currently is one of the most widely available and popular uromastyx species and also has been bred in captivity with some consistency by several breeders. Nevertheless, farmed babies often are sold as captive-bred, so be sure you purchase your lizard from a reputable source and treat the animal for worms if you suspect it came directly from Africa. (See also chapter 2 for a discussion on captive-bred versus imported specimens and chapter 6 for tips on parasite treatment and general health maintenance.) Future studies may show this form to be a subspecies of the African uromastyx.

## Egyptian Uromastyx

At 30 inches (76 cm) or perhaps more, *Uromastyx aegypticus* is the giant of the genus. Though babies may have distinct yellow spots or broken bands across the brown back, most adults are simply dark brown to blackish, without pattern, and dull yellowish brown on the belly. They have small,

A young Egyptian uro rests on its parent's head. *U. aegypticus* hatchlings are quite cute when they're still small enough to fit in your palm. Know, though, that they grow into large lizards that reach at least 30 inches (76 cm) from nose to tail tip, each adult requiring a cage about 6 feet (183 cm) long.

rounded heads compared with other uromastyx, and back scales that are almost too tiny and numerous (more than three hundred down the center of the back) to count. Additionally, the skin of the sides is strongly wrinkled, even in well-fed specimens. As previously mentioned, Egyptian uros make up in personality what they lack in color; they often can be very tame and pettable and won't struggle when picked up. Feed this species a highly varied diet, including colorful hibiscus and rose flowers, red clover, millet sprays, and cooked brown rice; some specimens even take alfalfa and timothy hay. Give insects only to young specimens. Though captive breeding is uncommon, captive-bred young are available. In this species, the male may be much more aggressive than the female, and females may be damaged during mating bouts. As a large lizard, it needs a very large vivarium to be comfortable—and a cage 6 feet (183 cm) long is not too big for a single adult. Be aware that although this species tends to be gentle, it has a strong, painful bite if irritated or surprised, and the spiny tail can scratch and draw blood.

## Ornate Uromastyx

This colorful species, *Uromastyx ornatus*, came onto the market by the thousands in the early 1990s (and still appears, though sporadically). Most were exported from Egypt, which has been reducing exports of reptiles, but for-

A docile temperament and striking color patterns as seen here have made the ornate uro one of the most popular species. *U. ornatus* usually are smaller than most species (rarely exceeding 12 inches, 30 cm long), making this species a good choice for beginning uro keepers.

tunately captive-bred young and even adults are now widely available, though expensive. Imported babies seldom adapt to the vivarium and may die in a few weeks. Unlike other common uromastyx, this species exhibits sexual dichromatism, a form of dimorphism ("two shapes") in which the sexes are of different colors. Adult females, even when warm, tend to be reddish brown with yellowish spots and short bands on the back. Adult males have a strong wash of blue or green over the sides of the body, the face, and often the entire back. Males also have larger femoral and preanal pores than females do, usually with waxy strings coming from the pores. Because of their relatively small size (seldom more than 12 inches, 30 cm) and sturdiness once adapted, plus a pleasing personality, the ornate uromastyx can make an excellent pet and, especially when captive-bred, perhaps is the best choice for beginners.

# CHAPTER 8

# AFRICAN AGAMIDS

A frica is not exactly crawling with a diverse fauna of agamid lizards, though it certainly has its share. Of the roughly fifty to sixty agamids found on the continent, along with a few dozen more in the Middle East, all can be placed in three genera: *Uromastyx*, which we've already talked about; the house agamas of genus *Agama* proper and some questionably distinct allied genera; and the bizarre little shield-tails of genus *Xenagama*, which are poorly known. All these genera share a liking for relatively dry, open country, though some species of *Agama* have become adapted to living in human villages and even larger cities over the continent.

Unfortunately, few species of African agamids other than the uromastyx are truly common in the vivarium hobby, though some house agamas and similar species can be found at low prices as imported specimens.

## House Agamas (Genus *Agama*)

*Agama* once was a gigantic genus found over most of Africa, the Middle East, and India, but it has been broken into four genera that are now generally recognized by herpetologists: *Agama*, *Laudakia*, *Pseudotrapelus*, and *Trapelus*. The latter three genera include species found in deep deserts and mountains mostly from northern Africa through the Middle East, and the genus *Agama* as now restricted comprises at least thirty species and many subspecies from Africa. These lizards have a heavy head and a moderately flattened back; the long tail is covered with overlapping spiny scales. As is true with most lizards, they have a visible ear drum (tympanum) and a fold of skin running across the throat. Males usually are much more colorful and larger than females, and they have preanal pores as well as pads of

thick, oddly shaped belly scales located approximately where you might look for a belly button.

Typical agamas are creatures of both the dry savannas and deserts of southern and eastern Africa and the more humid forest edges of western Africa, though none penetrate deeply into the Sahara and Namib deserts or the rain forests of the Congo basin. They vary in length from 6 to 16 inches (15 cm to 41 cm) and range from shy, solitary lizards specialized for feeding on ants to colonial omnivores able to live in native villages and gardens. Often, males are territorial, occupying a definite home range centered at a particular tree, rock, or wall and defending it against other males. Males may keep harems of several females and not allow nondominant males to mate. All house agamas lay eggs, usually six to twenty in a clutch laid in a nest burrow that the female digs in compact sandy soils. Incubation varies from two to four months depending on species and environment. Most species that appear in pet shops are wild-caught animals that may do well on a diet of crickets, greens, mixed fruits and vegetables, and the occasional pinkie mouse. Adults should not be kept with juveniles, which could be eaten.

The terrarium for house agamas should be large, at least 3 feet (91 cm) long, with a dry substrate of sand and soil and many climbing branches and rocks on which to bask. A well-secured screen lid is a must. Keep the air temperature at roughly 82°F (28°C), and provide a basking light to give a hot spot of about 100°F (38°C). Using a full-spectrum light supplying UV-B will help bring out the brightest colors of these lizards, increase their activity, and ensure good calcium and vitamin $D_3$ utilization.

## House or Red-Headed Agama

*Agama agama* is an interesting and often abundant African lizard sometimes imported in decent numbers that generally holds up well in the vivarium. The species is found over much of central Africa, from Ethiopia to Tanzania and west to the Atlantic Ocean. House agamas adapt well to the presence of humans and often establish themselves in villages and small cities near their natural habitat, where they can be seen sunning on house walls and trees. Though highly variable in coloration, males typically have a contrasting-colored pattern during the breeding season (the rainy season in Africa), with the head often bright golden yellow, orange, or red. The body usually is brown, often with a narrow pale stripe down the center of the back; the hind legs and tail may be iridescent blue. Males can reach 16 inches (41 cm) in length, whereas females reach about 12 inches (30 cm). Males have a low crest on the nape, small pores in front of the vent, and an aggressive attitude. Females lay three to six eggs in a burrow or in a nesting spot in a dead tree; the eggs hatch in sixty to ninety days when incubated at 85°F

Pictured here is a male red-headed agama (*Agama agama*) displaying bold colors. As temperatures drop during the night, the males typically take on a dull, brown appearance.

(29.5°C). Gravid females often develop bright orange stripes on the sides of the body and sometimes have small blue spots on the head and back. A surprising number of imported house agamas seen in shops are gravid females that will lay fertile eggs shortly after becoming adapted to the vivarium. Unfortunately, these females often die soon after laying from the stress of capture and shipment, though sometimes heavy supplements of calcium and vitamin $D_3$ and full-spectrum lighting may save them.

House agamas are a colonial yet territorial species, so keep only one male per vivarium and do not put small lizards with large ones. Give the lizards plenty of climbing branches as well as a hot basking spot opposite a cooler corner with a hide box on the substrate. As is usual with imported agamids, most wild specimens have serious infestations of intestinal worms and should be wormed by a knowledgeable veterinarian or experienced keeper. Mites and small ticks are also common and should be treated. Although house agamas get most of their water from their food, they will take water from a shallow dish or may be misted with lukewarm water a few times a week. Provide the usual salad greens and vegetables supplemented with crickets, mealworms, and waxworms; the insect portion should make up about a third of the total diet. House agamas can put on a lively chase to catch crickets and larger grasshoppers.

## Painted Agama

*Laudakia stellio* is widely known as the painted agama, but Europeans also call it by the native name, hardun. Genus *Laudakia* includes a few species of rather flattened agamas found from southeastern Europe across the Middle East into southern Asia. Formerly placed in *Agama*, they generally are terrestrial species with a large ear drum. One distinctive feature is that the scales on the tail are arranged in distinct whorls or rings, as opposed to the irregular arrangement found in *Agama* species.

The painted agama is found from northern Egypt over the Middle East and barely into southeastern Europe. Though variable (there are several subspecies), the species

This painted agama displays color rings around its tail characteristic of *Laudakia stellio.*

generally is easy to recognize by its rows of large or small golden yellow spots over the nearly black back and tail. Some individuals have large and conspicuous spots, whereas others may have only a few small spots; warm, acclimated painted agamas display much nicer coloration than the cool, stressed lizards you first see in the shops. The head is triangular and covered with large, often tuberculate scales, and the back features a mixture of large and small scales. Females display grayish bellies, and males are black or dark blue on the chest and throat. When ready to breed, dominant males may develop a bright blue color on their front legs. Adults are about 14 inches (36 cm) long from nose to tail tip, with the tail constituting more than half that length.

Painted agamas are a species native to dry, rocky areas and often are found on old fences and ruins at the edges of deserts and in dry, open woodlands. Mating follows a cooling period of eight to ten weeks at reduced temperatures (70°F, 21°C) and light. Each year, females lay several clutches of up to eight eggs in a nest hole that she digs in hard, sandy soil, so be sure to put a suitable nesting box with a mixture of sand, soil, and vermiculite in the vivarium. The eggs hatch in about fifty to sixty days if incubated at 85°F (29.5°C).

This agama often acclimates well to a vivarium and becomes quite tame, tolerating petting and being picked up. It may even learn to take a choice mealworm or bit of fruit from your fingers. Avoid imported specimens that are obviously dehydrated, have slack skin, lack fat at the base of the tail or have skinny legs, and are uninterested in defending themselves. Such specimens are probably sick and are likely to die. Provide a shallow water bowl and mist newly purchased pets; some may prefer water given from a dropper. After adapting to the vivarium, painted agamas will get most of their water from their food, but some still prefer a small water bowl. Don't let the humidity rise much higher than 70 percent, and be sure to provide full-spectrum light as well as a warm basking area.

## Shield-Tailed Agamas

In this unusual genus, *Xenagama* (literally, "strange agama"), are placed two poorly known species of small desert-dwelling agamids from Somalia and vicinity in eastern Africa: *Xenagama taylori* and *X. batillifera*. They look a bit like tiny uromastyx at first glance (in fact, *batillifera* was originally described in the genus *Uromastyx*) but they have less modified teeth typical of agamids and really are very close to species of the genus *Agama*. The head is large and boxy with large external ear openings, and the body is depressed. Typically, the dorsal scales are mixed sizes, some projecting as small cones. The tail is short—only half the length of the head and body—distinctly flattened and wide at the base, tapering to a more normal thin tip. The scales on the wide part of the tail are large and pointed, with those at the sides of the tail often projecting as long spines. Adults seldom reach more than 4 inches (10 cm) in length. They are burrowers in dry soils in a few mountain ranges of the Somali area. Until the turn of the century, the existence of shield-tailed agamids was virtually unknown to herpetologists. They have recently become available to hobbyists in small numbers. Though these lizards have proved delicate in the vivarium so far, some hobbyists have had good luck keeping and even breeding them, so they just may have a future in the hobby as "mini-uromastyx."

Both species have been imported, but at the moment the most common species seems to be *X. taylori*, sometimes called the turnip-tailed agama. In this species, the flattened

The beaver-tailed or Somali strange agama (*Xenagama batillifera*) is a small, quick lizard.

The turnip-tailed or Taylor's strange agama (*X. taylori*) has a shorter, rounder tail than its cousin *X. batillifera* shown above.

base of the tail is wide and disklike, projecting beyond the width of the trunk; it is usually at least 20 mm (almost an inch) wide in adults. The scales at the edges of the widened portion of the tail are extremely spiny, as are the other scales on the base of the tail. Adults are brownish with darker and paler brown spots and specks. Males develop a bright blue chest and throat, and the color may extend upward over the lips and even the snout. In females, there is at best a tinge of blue on a creamy tan background in this area.

The beaver-tailed agama, *Xenagama batillifera*, has a tail that is narrower at the base than in *X. taylori*—about 15 mm (about half an inch) wide in adults. The flattened base is covered with enlarged and spiny scales, but not to the extent of its cousin's; and the tail base tapers more uniformly to a narrow extension than it does in *X. taylori*, thus making the tail less disklike. The beaver-tailed agama is sandy tan to grayish above, with blackish spots or broken lines on the back in females; males have a blue throat and chest, with a tail that is yellow underneath.

You can keep both species in much the same way: in dry vivaria about 3 feet (91 cm) long with a substrate of play sand. Provide a small area of compact sandy soil and scatter some pebbles about. Give these lizards a hide box and a few rocks or pieces of bark under which to burrow and hide. The ambient temperature should be about 90°F (32°C), with a hot basking area kept close to 120°F (49°C) for much of the day. Provide full-spectrum light and keep the relative humidity low.

Feed these odd little agamids much as you would a house agama. Supply a green salad with additional vegetables, plus crickets, mealworms, and waxworms. These lizards may sip water from a shallow bowl, but they generally get the water they need from the foods that they eat.

Males apparently collect a harem of several females; however, if just a pair is kept together, the female may become aggressive toward the male. Unless you are willing to keep a close eye on your lizards at all times, it might be best to house each separately until the male's colors intensify to indicate he is ready to mate. A cooling period of sixty days may improve the chance of breeding. Females lay about six to ten eggs that hatch in about forty to fifty days when incubated at about 84°F (29°C), but breeding success has so far been limited, and most success has been with the turnip-tail. This limited breeding success coupled with the unstable political situation in Somalia and adjacent areas may mean that we will lose these fascinating agamids from the hobby.

# CHAPTER 9

# ASIAN AGAMIDS

Asia has a much more diverse fauna of agamid lizards than does Africa. Many genera found in the rain forests of Southeast Asia are of potential interest to hobbyists. Rather surprisingly, few of these often attractive and interesting lizards have proven to possess any staying power in the trade, and only the water dragons are likely to be found in most pet shops. Other Asian agamids are imported on a sporadic basis; they are seldom bred in captivity, and they long have been considered delicate and hard to keep. Currently, these lizards are much more popular in Germany than in the United States, but even in Germany they seldom are bred in great numbers.

It is not uncommon to find unidentified or misidentified Asian agamids in pet shops and at reptile expos. These imports arrive in large numbers for a few months or years and then virtually disappear from the hobby when no one succeeds in breeding them. These lizards usually are greatly stressed, carry large parasite loads, and are dehydrated. If they have no obvious wounds or broken bones, they may respond well to a warm vivarium after being wormed and rehydrated, much as you would treat a wild-caught uromastyx.

## Mountain Dragons

Included in this group (genera *Acanthosaura* and *Gonocephalus*) are interesting lizards from Southeast Asia and Indonesia that have been appearing for sale in some numbers for the past decade. Some of the larger species of *Gonocephalus* have high crests on the nape and are spectacular when seen in a suitably planted vivarium. Unfortunately, few thrive in the vivarium, and even fewer are successfully bred—but they certainly are not hopeless cases.

## Prickle-Napes

In the genus *Acanthosaura* are about four species of slender, long-tailed, long-legged, forest-dwelling agamids found from Myanmar (Burma) to Indonesia and southern China. They have commonly been called mountain horned dragons. That name is also used for species of related genera, so I prefer prickle-napes, a common name widely used in Europe. The wedge-shaped head has large eyes, often set in a dark brown to blackish mask, and set off above by very strong ridges: the "eyebrows." A series of high spines runs from about between the eyes onto at least the nape of the neck and sometimes well onto the back. Distinctive for the group are the prickles, a large isolated spine on each side of the head above and behind the eye near the end of the eyebrow—and usually a second spine just above the ear drum. Colors vary from brown to greenish with brown patterns, but stressed specimens often are almost uniformly black. The species look much alike, differing in details of color patterns and spines on the head and back, but the species most often seen are the diamond-backed prickle-nape (*Acanthosaura crucigera*) and the brown prickle-nape (*A. capra*), both from mountain forests in Southeast Asia.

Prickle-napes are rain forest lizards of high mountains in the tropics, usually staying in the trees, hugging the trunk or branches. They also spend much time on the ground, where they feed on an assortment of insects and other

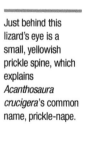

Just behind this lizard's eye is a small, yellowish prickle spine, which explains *Acanthosaura crucigera*'s common name, prickle-nape.

invertebrates, including earthworms. Males, which have a pair of distinctly swollen hemipene pouches under the base of the tail, are quite territorial and may be impossible to house together.

These lizards can be kept in a tall, humid vivarium, especially one that is heavily planted and has a small waterfall. A fiberglass mesh cage designed for use with chameleons works well, as it gives the lizards height to climb. Aim for a vivarium at least 3 feet (91 cm) high and long. Because most of these lizards don't know that standing water is drinkable, they must be misted daily with lukewarm water and also provided with a drip waterer, such as is used for chameleons. You also can try running an air line tube from a small air pump outside the vivarium into a shallow bowl of water with an air stone; the air turns the water into mist that attracts the lizard. Prickle-napes do not need very warm enclosure temperatures. They do best when kept between 70°F and 80°F (21°C and 26.5°C); temperatures higher than 84°F (29°C) are stressful and may lead to death if maintained for several weeks. Prickle-napes do not bask and thus need neither basking lamps nor full-spectrum lighting (though it wouldn't hurt). Aim for a relative humidity of 70 percent, highest near the bottom of the vivarium; a moisture-retaining substrate such as orchid bark or cypress mulch works well. An over-wintering (or brumation) period at lower temperature and humidity may be necessary for long-term success, though some keepers have had good luck without varying the temperature and humidity. Captives will take crickets, mealworms, silkworms, waxworms, and other insects, and some may even capture earthworms and an occasional fish when offered in a shallow dish. Prickle-napes are considered delicate in captivity and often do poorly, but this probably is because so many imports are badly stressed and then kept much too warm and too dry to ever acclimate. Gravid imports may occasionally lay their eggs in deep nesting boxes when provided with a moist substrate.

The diamond-backed prickle-nape (*A. crucigera*) is the most colorful species seen. Adults are 8 to 12 inches (20 to

30 cm) long, the male longer than the female, and have high spines over both the eye and tympanum. A distinctive pattern of this species is a large black diamond on the nape that is connected at the sides to an oblique black slash over the front legs. This usually is a brownish lizard that sometimes takes on a greenish tinge, especially in females. It is more terrestrial than usual for the genus and often is found foraging on the ground, taking refuge in the trees when threatened. Females may lay a dozen eggs that hatch in five or six months when incubated at a temperature that stays between about 65°F and 75°F (18°C and 24°C) and at a relatively low humidity of just 60 percent.

Less colorful but currently more available is the brown prickle-nape (*A. capra*), which generally is an overall mottled dark and light brown with some green patches and spots. This species is a bit longer than the diamond-backed (males often a foot, 30 cm, long) and lacks the spine over the ear drum. It has been bred in small numbers in captivity.

## Angleheads

The fifteen to twenty species of the genus *Gonocephalus* are the giants of the mountain dragons, with some species exceeding 16 inches (41 cm) in length and having very high, deeply compressed bodies similar at first glance to many chameleons. They vary greatly in details of color, body form, and spines, but all have a very heavy, boxy head marked by

The eyes are a fairly reliable sex indicator among anglehead lizards. Males, such as the *Gonocephalus grandis* shown here, have blue eyes (rarely, orange) whereas females usually have orange eyes.

thick, high ridges over the eyes that run forward to the tip of the snout. These ridges often end in prominent triangular spines. There may be crests of very large, compressed spines on the nape, with lower spines running down the center of the back toward the tail. Angleheads usually have a large, obvious gular crest (a rounded fold of skin hanging below the throat similar to the crest in a male anole), and in males this crest may be especially large. The legs are long and strong, and the tail (which may be quite slender) is about double the length of the body. Color patterns vary, but generally these are green to brown lizards with a pattern of pale crossbands over the back. The bands may be widened and connected along the center of the back or reduced to small dark spots. Angleheads are found in forests, usually near water, from the southern Malayan Peninsula over the Indonesian islands and the Philippines. Very similar but usually larger species of angleheads found in New Guinea and northern Australia now commonly are placed in the genus *Hypsilurus*, which cannot be told from *Gonocephalus* externally.

Angleheads sometimes appear in the hobby as imports, which are hard to maintain for any length of time. They need a tall, large, heavily planted vivarium similar to one for the prickle-napes. The enclosure should be humid but well ventilated and should be kept fairly warm (not higher than 85°F, 29.5°C); a mesh chameleon vivarium works well. Like prickle-napes, angleheads recognize only moving water, so use a drip system like that for chameleons, mist daily, or run an air line into the water bowl. Usually, angleheads rest at the ends of thin branches, which makes them difficult to collect in nature. Most species appear to be relatively non-territorial, and it has been suggested that several species or even pairs of one species may be kept together if the vivarium is large enough; but they are best housed separately. Angleheads feed on large insects (grasshoppers, crickets, beetles, moths, and the like) and sometimes on small lizards, frogs, and baby mice (live or prekilled).

Often the entire eye color of the male is bright blue, and that of the female may be bright orange, but males of some species have orange eyes. Males are distinguished from females by greater development of the spines and the presence of swollen hemipene pouches at the base of the tail. Females lay up to half a dozen eggs in litter near the base of their home tree, and she may lay several clutches a year. Incubation is similar to that of the prickle-nape and may take three to four months. Seldom do these dragons reproduce successfully in the vivarium.

Several species, often not identifiable, have been imported in the past, but probably Abbott's anglehead (*Gonocephalus doriae*) is the species most often seen. This species is found from mountain forests of Thailand into the Malayan Peninsula. Male Abbott's angleheads are reddish brown and have a blue ring in the eye whereas juveniles and females typically are green. The large compressed spines on the nape are in just two overlapping rows; in males, the nape itself is swollen into a semicircle accentuating the crest.

## Garden Lizards

Widely known both as "blood suckers" (because of the red lips of the males in some species) and as "beauty lizards," the garden lizards (genus *Calotes*) are agamid versions of the American anoles (genus *Anolis*). Twenty or more *Calotes* species commonly are recognized, with many being difficult to distinguish. They usually can be recognized by their compressed form (flattened from side to side) and the presence

A beauty lizard (*Calotes* sp.) perches on a tree branch. These agamas are sometimes called blood suckers, though the name is typically used for specimens that display red lips.

of large, shinglelike scales of uniform size on the back. A crest of spines runs from the nape to the tail, and it may be especially well developed on the nape in males of many species. There may be spinous scales at the back of the head or over the eye (somewhat similar to prickle-napes), and the ear drum is clearly visible. The tail is compressed and commonly at least three times the body length, which in adults is 8 to 16 inches (20 to 41 cm).

Garden lizards display a variety of colors, from nearly gray to bright green and often with red or blue on the head. A pattern of dark brown spots or triangles on the sides may be present. There is much variation within a species due to age, sex, and mood, with the males especially able to quickly change colors. Garden lizards appear in many habitats from Iran and across India to southern China, then south over Southeast Asia and the Indonesian islands.

Most garden lizards are arboreal and prefer open, relatively dry forests and shrubby areas. There they can spend the day basking in sunlight and chasing insects between bouts of territorial defense and mating. Males cannot be kept together, and even two or three females may not be compatible in smaller vivaria. They need a large vivarium with many climbing areas, such as clumps of artificial plants and branches. A basking light is essential, as is a full-spectrum light. Daily misting and a bowl of water are both required. Food should consist of crickets, grasshoppers, and larger insects (such as moths and butterflies), as well as mealworms and waxworms—but many species actually prefer smaller lizards as the principal prey, so keeping mixed groups of lizards in the same setup is not encouraged. Few garden lizards are bred in captivity, and wild-caught specimens are nervous, parasitized, and stressed, often unable to adapt to captive conditions. Few garden lizards survive more than two or three months to a year in captivity, so they have a poor reputation among hobbyists. In nature, females lay clutches of four to twelve eggs in the litter, which hatch into brownish young in two to three months.

The turquoise garden lizard (*Calotes mystaceus*) seems to be imported with some regularity of late. It is a large but slender species, 14 to 16 inches (35 to 31 cm) long, with a high, very spiny nape crest that in males continues onto the back. In good color, males are grayish with a strong iridescent blue tinge on the face and sides. There are a few large brown spots paired on the anterior body, as well as a broad white stripe that runs from the tip of the snout along the upper lip to above the front leg. This species is common near villages and in cultivated areas over much of Southeast Asia from Myanmar (Burma) to Vietnam.

## Hydrosaurs

The genus *Hydrosaurus*, known as hydrosaurs or sailfin dragons, includes at least four species of strange agamids from tropical southern Asia. These heavy-bodied lizards, often nearly 40 inches (a meter) long, are long-legged, long-toed, semiaquatic agamids found from the Philippines and Indonesian islands to New Guinea. Adults have large heads with rather bulbous snouts and large eyebrow ridges. Running from the nape of the neck down the back to the base of the tail is a high crest of spiny scales connected by thick skin; the crest continues onto the compressed tail as the sail, and in males it may be much higher than the fleshy part of the tail. There are lobes of free skin on the elongated fingers and toes, and males have femoral and preanal pores. Most hydrosaurs are pale brown to greenish above, whitish below, with irregular darker brown lines on

The "sail" of sailfin dragons (shown here is a male *Hydrosaurus amboinensis*) is a crest composed of spiny scales connected by thick skin.

the back. Breeding males may become yellowish orange over the body and belly, with bright blue highlights on the head and with blue or red eyes. Few lizards are more impressive than adult hydrosaurs.

Hydrosaurs are large lizards that are difficult to acclimate and seldom are bred in captivity. In nature, they are found in or over jungle streams, taking to the water when disturbed. They often bask on a branch over the water and drop down to escape by swimming away. In captivity, hydrosaurs require a vivarium at least 6 feet (183 cm) long and nearly as high, with a large portion of the base covered with shallow water; a greenhouse obviously would work better than a cage, so adults seldom can be kept indoors in the typical home. The vivarium should be kept warm and moist, but a basking light is not required. In nature, these lizards feed mostly on leaves and fruits, preferring brightly colored foods, but they also take frogs, lizards, insects, and other meaty foods. Be careful: the front teeth in the upper jaw are enlarged into sabers and can produce a nasty bite. Hydrosaurs need supplemental vitamins and calcium and full-spectrum lights.

A few captive-bred hydrosaurs are available, but wild-caught juveniles often are offered. Most specimens seen are *Hydrosaurus amboinensis*, the common or Ambon sailfin, which ranges from southern Indonesia to western New Guinea and the southern Philippines. Because of their size and the potential danger involved in keeping these lizards, they are not recommended for beginners.

## Water Dragons

At last we come to a pair of quite keepable (though large) Asian agamids that are available as captive-bred specimens if you look around for them a bit. These are the water dragons, genus *Physignathus*, two of the larger species (perhaps not really related to each other) of agamids. Brown water dragons (*Physignathus lesueuri*) are found from New Guinea into eastern Australia and usually are brown with traces of oblique paler bands on the sides, and sometimes with bright cream lips. Though this species is fairly available

A male green water dragon (*Physignathus cocincinus*) grasps a branch to balance his body. Captive specimens need adequate room to climb, which requires tall vivaria—about 6 feet (183 cm) for adults.

and is captive-bred, its dull colors help prevent it from becoming a more familiar pet. Its care and to some extent natural history are much like that of the green water dragon.

Green water dragons (*P. cocincinus*) are also familiarly called Chinese water dragons, and they actually do range over much of Southeast Asia north into southern China. Often confused with the green iguana (*Iguana iguana*), this 40-inch (1 meter) agamid stays some shade of green or blue green throughout life and has a very long tail (accounting for two-thirds of the total length) that is banded in black and white. The head is marked by high bony ridges over the golden eyes, and the scales of the lower lip usually are pinkish to white, with several distinctive conical white scales behind the jaws; this species does not have a large round scale below the ear drum as seen in the green iguana. Young specimens often have narrow white oblique bands on the sides, whereas old adults may have brilliant pink lips and bright yellow chests, and some adults are distinctly blue. Like many agamids, the green water dragon has long legs and long toes, an adaptation to living in dense forests where it climbs trunks and branches over jungle streams. A common defense behavior is to drop into the water when challenged and swim to safety. In both sexes, a crest of narrow spines runs from the nape of the neck down the center of the back onto the tail.

Keeping a young green water dragon can be difficult, as they are relatively delicate and flighty lizards notorious for panicking and banging their snouts on the vivarium glass. Most babies sold are wild-caught or farmed imports; if not especially stressed or dehydrated, they acclimate well. Give a baby green water dragon the largest vivarium you can afford, remembering that in two or three years the lizard might exceed 3 feet (91 cm) in length and will want to climb and have a large water basin in its cage. These are arboreal lizards that are almost semiaquatic; this dictates how their vivarium must be set up. Try to provide a tall vivarium at least 3 feet (91 cm) high for babies; adults need a cage about 4 to 6 feet (122 to 183 cm) high. The bottom of the vivarium should be covered with a moisture-holding substrate such as orchid bark or cypress mulch and should include a water basin larger than half the length of the lizard and deep enough to allow the dragon to submerge. Include several climbing branches and some plastic plants to replicate nature. Keep the vivarium between 80°F and 85°F (26.5°C and 29.5°C) at all times, allowing only a small temperature drop at night; temperatures below 60°F (16°C) may be fatal. Also essential are a full-spectrum light as a UV-B source and a weak basking light positioned over a favorite branch. Mist the vivarium daily, and maintain a relative humidity of about 70 percent.

Feeding a green water dragon is easy, as they are omnivores that favor small animal prey over plants. Roughly two-thirds of the diet should consist of meaty foods— crickets, mealworms, superworms (for adults), waxworms, green cockroaches, grasshoppers, beetles, small frogs, fish, and even baby mice. The other third of the diet should be a good green salad with some chopped fruits added. The size of the food pieces should match the size of the lizard's open mouth. Some individuals prefer greens, but most will take their insects before even glancing at their salad.

Breeding these large, very active lizards in captivity is difficult and requires access to large quarters such as a greenhouse. Males are larger than females, have much higher crests, and have swollen jowls; they also have enlarged femoral pores compared with females. Courtship may include the male chasing the female through the branches, followed by holding her in place with a bite to the nape and then mating. A month or more later, the female lays half a dozen to a dozen large, white eggs in a nest hole dug in the substrate. These hatch after two to three months when incubated at 75°F to 85°F (24°C to 29.5°C) and 70 percent humidity. House each baby separately to prevent fighting. The young require calcium and vitamin $D_3$ supplements as well as a good source of UV-B light if they are to grow well and not develop metabolic bone disease.

Green water dragons have many advantages over green iguanas (including not being restricted to a vegetarian diet, being somewhat smaller, and not becoming aggressive when adult), but they can be too nervous for their own good, especially when young. However, once they are about half grown, they calm down and make excellent pets that can tolerate handling and even a bit of laxity about vivarium conditions. Consider this species as not just an alternative to green iguanas but a definite improvement.

# CHAPTER 10

# AUSTRALIAN AGAMIDS

Agamids are abundant in Australia, with more than sixty species housed in more than a dozen genera. Only a few of these species extend northward into New Guinea, and only a few New Guinea agamids (such as the genera *Hypsilurus* and *Chlamydosaurus*) are shared with Australia. (Australasia, incidentally, is a term applied to Australia plus New Guinea and outlying islands, all of which once were part of a single large continent that only recently has begun breaking apart.) Many Australian lizards would make great pets if they were available, but Australia has greatly restricted or forbidden exportation of its reptiles since at least 1970. Only a few species have been able to successfully remain in the hobby over this time through captive breeding or because of their presence in western New Guinea, a territory of Indonesia that allows sale of its fauna. Only the frilled dragon from New Guinea and the extremely popular bearded dragon from Australia can be said to be familiar Australasian agamids.

## Frilled Dragons

Since it was used as a model for the "cute" venom-spitting dinosaur *Dilophosaurus* in the film *Jurassic Park*, the frilled dragon has seen its popularity increase, though it is not suitable for beginners. *Chlamydosaurus kingi* is a slender, long-legged and long-tailed agamid that may reach 3 feet (91 cm) in length and is found in dry forests of southern New Guinea and across northern Australia. It is immediately recognizable by the frill of loose skin that forms a nearly complete umbrella around the head, being divided only on the nape of the neck. The frill is connected to supporting structures in the lizard's throat and spreads

This frilled dragon (*Chlamydosaurus kingi*) assumes a defensive or threat posture.

widely when the lizard opens its mouth. Bright pinkish mouth membranes contrast with the grayish or brownish frill, which may carry some orange or yellow spots and patches. The frill is unique among living agamids and is present at hatching, though it is much smaller in babies than it is in old males.

In nature, frilled dragons inhabit dry forests in the tropics and are found both on the ground and basking on branches. They are famous for running away from predators while standing on their hind legs, often called "bicycling." For some obscure reason, frilled dragons and their running style became a short-lived popular fad in Japan a few years ago, and images of frilled dragons appeared everywhere, including on clothing and toys. Today, frills are fairly common in the vivarium hobby, often being seen as babies and subadults that are imported from western New Guinea, where they may be locally farmed. Specimens cannot be imported legally from Australia or eastern New Guinea, but the species has been captive-bred domestically for at least a decade. This lizard often is purchased on impulse, but consider purchases carefully to be sure you will be able to give frilled dragons the attention and environment they need. These lizards grow to a large size and need large quarters when adult. Though many adults are hand-tame and seldom are vicious, they can scratch and can give a painful bite.

Young frilled dragons can be kept in large aquaria with the proper lighting, other necessities as listed below, and some climbing branches. However, they quickly outgrow most aquaria, so save yourself the trouble and establish them in a large vivarium from the beginning. Adult males reach a length of almost 3 feet (91 cm) and females about 2 feet (61 cm) by two or three years of age. These lizards are partially arboreal, so you need a vivarium at least 4 feet (122 cm) long and as close to 3 feet (91 cm) high as possible to make them comfortable. Use a fairly deep substrate that holds some moisture, such as orchid bark or cypress mulch, and place a shallow water basin at least 2 feet (61 cm) long at the bottom. If possible, put a small undertank heating pad under the basin (outside the vivarium, of course) so the water stays warm; replace the water daily, as the lizards tend to defecate in the water as well as drink it and soak in it. Wedge several broad branches into the vivarium that will allow the frills to lounge under a weak basking light (about 100°F, 38°C, at the hottest spot). You want to try to maintain a temperature of roughly 80°F (26.5°C) near the bottom of the vivarium. A pair of full-spectrum fluorescent tubes producing at least 2 percent UV-B light should run the length of the vivarium. Be sure the vivarium is securely screened on top so the lizards, which are strong climbers, cannot reach the bulbs and be burned.

Feeding frilled dragons usually is simple, as they take a great variety of animal foods. Be sure the size of the food matches the mouth of the lizard—babies can take mealworms, for instance, yet adults might prefer frozen and thawed whole adult mice. Try to feed as many different foods as possible: crickets, mealworms, superworms, waxworms, butterworms (also called tebos), cultured cockroaches, small frogs and lizards (adults may eat their young,

Hatchling frilled dragons survey their enclosure from a perch. The yellow areas near their necks are their tiny frills in the relaxed position.

so be careful), and mice of all sizes, preferably prekilled. Use calcium and vitamin $D_3$ supplements on the food, especially for growing young, and feed crickets and mealworms gutloading foods to make sure they have a high nutritional content. Some frilled dragons can become "hooked" on a certain food item and not accept anything else, so alternate types of food over the week. Babies generally are fed each day, whereas adults are fed two or three times a week. Many frilled dragons will learn to take food from your fingers (start by offering it at the tips of forceps—a frill bite can draw blood) and become very tame as long as they are handled during each feeding. Wild frilled dragons tend to be nervous and can scratch.

Breeding frilled dragons requires a lot of room, as the male may chase the female in the vivarium, and two lizards each almost 3 feet (91 cm) long moving through a cage can be quite destructive to the landscape. Females mature when roughly thirty months old, whereas males are fully mature a bit later. In their natural habitat, frilled dragons breed after several months of dormancy induced by dry conditions. So in the vivarium, you have to give them a similar dormancy period. To keep the lizards more or less aligned with natural seasons, start the cooling period in August. Over about two weeks, gradually drop the temperature to 65°F to 70°F (18°C to 21°C), remove the water, stop feeding, and turn off the lights. Do this in steps to make sure that the intestines of the lizards are empty and that they have passed their last meals into their water basin as normal. Any frilled dragon put into a summer dormancy must be perfectly healthy and have good fat stores on the body because it will lose significant weight during the next eight to twelve weeks without feeding. After the dormancy period, bring the lizards back to normal temperature and light conditions, start feeding heavily, and simulate rains—heavy rains. You can mist the vivarium several times a day, let the frills soak in their water basins, and, if possible, spray them with a hose. This allows them not only to drink their fill but also to believe that the breeding rains have come. Mating should follow shortly after the lizards are put together.

Males are larger and have heavier heads and longer frills than females do. They also have obvious hemipene pouches at the base of the tail. They are aggressive and will obviously stalk females. The female may try to avoid the male but is always caught and mated. A single male will mate with many females over several months, but it is always safest to put one pair together at a time. Females lay at least half a dozen large, white eggs in a nest hole dug in soft, moist substrate (a deep, plastic nest box filled with a sand and vermiculite mix works well). The eggs hatch after almost three months when incubated at roughly 84°F (29°C) and at 90 percent humidity.

Though babies are social, they will sometimes fight and are best separated. Be sure they have access to a large, shallow water bowl at all times, as well as UV-B lighting, lots of calcium and vitamin $D_3$, and a variety of insect foods.

## Bearded Dragons

The one great success of agamid lizards in the vivarium has been the inland bearded dragon (*Pogona vitticeps*), a great pet lizard that has been widely kept and bred in Europe and

In a defense or threat posture, this inland bearded dragon (*Pogona vitticeps*) displays a full "beard."

the United States for about thirty years. Most pet shops that handle reptiles offer bearded dragons. At a reptile expo, you might see red and yellow varieties produced commercially through selective breeding as well as the normal brown and cream dragons. Bearded dragons are nearly perfect pets if you don't mind having to provide a large vivarium (preferably at least 40 inches, 1 meter, long for a single large specimen) and warm basking lights (at least 100°F, 38°C). Not that "beardies" are simple pets—some can be aggressive toward other bearded dragons and if startled can bite and scratch you (though not badly). A major problem is that some dealers sell bearded babies when they are too young (just out of the egg); these babies don't adapt well. If possible, buy a bearded dragon that is already half-grown.

Adult inland bearded dragons commonly are 18 inches (46 cm) long or longer and are heavy-bodied with a depressed body type. They have large heads, fairly short snouts, and large eyes. The legs are not exceptionally long and are well-muscled compared with some other agamids with pencil-thin legs, and the tail is fairly long and muscular. The first thing you will notice about a bearded dragon is the spines—the entire body and tail are covered with short, flexible spines that become quite long at the sides of the body and at the back corners of the head. Under the throat is an expandable sac with long points on the scales; when expanded, the scale points bristle-out and become the "beard." There is a dark stripe back from the eye to the ear drum—the "*vitticeps*" (or "striped head") of the scientific name. The open mouth often is bright orange, a scary color when you first see it. Wild-colored beardies are pale tan with a darker brown or gray mottled and spotted pattern, but several colors and patterns also are available to today's hobbyists. Males are larger than females and are usually more aggressive. Males have large, open femoral pores under the hind legs (smaller and generally not open in females), larger heads, and black throats.

These lizards vary from terrestrial to somewhat arboreal and are found naturally in dry savannas and in open eucalyptus forests of eastern Australia, where they often are seen chasing insects through the tops of low shrubs. These agamids do well on a sandy substrate with a hide box in a cool corner of the vivarium and a log or rock on which to bask under a basking light (100°F, 38°C). Try to keep the vivarium at roughly 90°F (32°C) in the warmest corner and at 75°F (24°C) near the hide box. Provide full-spectrum light over a screen cover that the lizard cannot lift. Many beardies like to climb and will use climbing branches, but others are perfectly at home on the ground. Water can be given in a shallow bowl that is changed daily.

Feeding is easy, as bearded dragons take mostly insects of all types. Adult beardies also will take small prekilled mice. Give crickets and waxworms as the major diet. (Mealworms and superworms are good for adults, but not for baby lizards, as the worms may cause paralysis. One of the mysteries of dragons, feeding mealworms to baby dragons causes paralysis, which is sometimes fatal, and no one has any idea why.) Frozen and thawed mice of appropriate size can be offered once a week, or less frequently as a treat. Feed at least three times a week. Once or twice a week, offer a mixed salad of greens and chopped fruits because beardies really are omnivores. Some bearded dragons will not take plant foods, but others love their salads. As usual, try to give the greatest variety possible of both plant and animal foods. Remember to provide calcium and vitamin $D_3$ supplements for both growing babies and gravid females.

House hatchling beardies individually (or at most three or four per cage) to prevent fighting.

Breeding is relatively easy, though it is best if the breeding cage is at least 4 feet (122 cm) long so the lizards can run as the female tries to escape the male. Mating occurs after a three-month cooling period when the temperature is allowed to drop to 65°F (18°C) over two weeks, the lighting is reduced to just a few hours a day, and food is withdrawn. Keep water available to the lizards during the cooling period, and house the sexes separately. Feed the lizards well when they come back to regular temperature and light conditions, mist them frequently, and let them soak if they wish (most don't). Mating is rough, and females may be injured during the battle, suffering deep bites that, fortunately, heal well. The female lays as many as two dozen eggs in a moist nest box about two months after mating. These hatch in sixty days when incubated at 85°F (29.5°C). The babies tend to fight, so separate them into small groups or keep them individually to prevent injuries entirely. Never feed mealworms to baby bearded dragons—the worms definitely have caused temporary and even terminal paralysis in beardies that are only a few inches long.

# RESOURCES

## Books

Cox, M. J., et al. *A Photographic Guide to Snakes and Other Reptiles of Peninsular Malaysia, Singapore and Thailand.* Sanibel Island, Fla.: Ralph Curtis Books, 1998.

De Vosjoli, P. *Green Water Dragons.* Mission Viejo, Calif.: Advanced Vivarium Systems, 1992.

De Vosjoli, P., Robert Mailloux, Susan Donoghue, Roger Klingenberg, and Jerry Cole. *The Bearded Dragon Manual.* Mission Viejo, Calif.: Advanced Vivarium Systems, 2001.

Walls, J. G. *Best Reptile Pets.* Neptune City, N.J.: T.F.H. Publ., 2001.

## Magazine Articles

Bartlett, R. D. "Thoughts on the Little-Known Shield-Tailed Agama, *Xenagama taylori.*" *Reptile & Amphibian Hobbyist* (November 2001): 20–28.

Bradley, M. E. "The New Dragon on the Horizon [*Acanthosaura*]." *Reptiles* (October 2003): 76–84.

Gray, R. L. "Captive Husbandry of Ornate Spiny-Tailed Lizards." *Reptiles* (July 1995): 64–77.

Gray, R. L. and W. Walsh. "Unearthing Uromastyx: The Newly Described Mali Spiny-Tailed Lizard." *Reptiles* (February 1998): 40–45.

Leslie, A. V. "Captive Care of Uromastyx Lizards." *Reptiles* (July 2003): 48–62.

Pike, L. "Desert Delights." *Reptiles USA Annual* 10 (2005): 100–107.

Weis, P. "Thrills, Chills & Frills." *Reptiles* (April 2003): 48–63.

## Web Sites

**http://www.reptilesmagazine.com**
The Web site for *Reptiles* magazine, including links, species profiles, and interesting tidbits.

**http://www.kingsnake.com**
Excellent commercial site with links to many specialty groups and clubs, as well as care sheets and dealers, reptile expo calendars, and discussion groups. Over twenty-two million visitors.

# INDEX

# ABOUT THE AUTHOR

A native of central Louisiana, **Jerry Walls** worked as an editor in New Jersey for more than thirty years, authoring more than four hundred publications on natural history subjects, especially reptiles and amphibians. His thirty-eight books (including twenty on herps) range from introductory works on lizards and turtles as pets to massive reviews of seashells, boas and pythons, and poisonous frogs. He also edited *Reptile Hobbyist* magazine and currently writes a monthly column for *Reptiles* magazine. He is an active birder, with more than six hundred U.S. species on his life list, and has authored several books and articles on pet and wild birds. Collecting crawfishes, snails, and herps for taxonomic study currently is his favorite preoccupation.